THE NEW
MATHEMATICS
IN OUR SCHOOLS

A Macmillan Guidebook for Parents

Donovan A. Johnson

Robert Rahtz

THE NEW MATHEMATICS IN OUR SCHOOLS

The Macmillan Company   NEW YORK

Collier-Macmillan Limited   LONDON

Library of Congress catalog card number: 66–14207

THE MACMILLAN COMPANY, NEW YORK
COLLIER-MACMILLAN CANADA, LTD., TORONTO, ONTARIO

Printed in the United States of America

PREFACE

Mathematics is now the hero on the academic stage. Suddenly we have become aware of the importance of mathematics in our society. One can hardly escape reading about the great demand for more scientists, mathematicians, teachers, and engineers with a strong mathematics background. Legislation involving science and mathematics is virtually an everyday event. Similarly, the interests of citizens, scholars, and teachers about present mathematics instruction are reflected in the many articles about it and the many commissions and committees studying the mathematics and science curriculums. This, then, is the setting for the new school mathematics.

Mathematics has been often ignored and more often disliked by the typical parent, pupil, and teacher. We usually think of mathematics as a technical field of use only to the scientist or engineer. Few people realize that mathematics is a vast, changing field of knowledge which is playing a major role in molding our modern culture. Few students realize that the study of mathematics can be a pleasant, satisfying experience. Few teachers realize that teaching mathematics can be an exciting adventure. Few parents realize that learning the new mathematics with their children can be a recreation. It is the purpose of this book to build an understanding of and appreciation for the new school mathematics.

We will attempt to answer questions such as these about the new school mathematics: **1385051**

1. What is the new school mathematices?
2. Why do we need new mathematics in our schools?
3. How did the new mathematics get into our schools?
4. What are some of the exciting new ideas of the new mathematics?
5. How can I help my child if he is studying the new mathematics?
6. Are the students in new mathematics programs learning more mathematics than students of traditional programs?

This book provides answers to these and other questions. At the same time we will of necessity do a good deal of teaching of the new mathematics. We attempt to orient you to the new content and its teaching so that you will have some basic understanding of what the new mathematics is all about. When you have finished this book, we hope you will be sufficiently interested to pursue the field on your own. We provide a bibliography of books that are suitable for independent study of mathematics.

In developing the subject we write informally. We do not assume a knowledge of mathematics beyond what is normally taught in the eighth grade. The new topics are presented in such a way as to convey the flavor of the new mathematics.

The primary purpose of this book is not to make you an expert in the new mathematics but to help you learn new ideas about mathematics so that you will better appreciate what your youngster is doing in his mathematics classes.

It is always embarrassing and destructive to a parent's ego if he is unable to fathom what his youngster is doing in school. We hope to spare you this experience.

D. A. J.
R. R.

CONTENTS

THE NEW
MATHEMATICS
IN OUR SCHOOLS

WHY NEW MATHEMATICS IN OUR SCHOOLS?

1

Most of us think of mathematics as an ancient science dealing with ideas that never change. Even though most people realize vaguely that mathematics is a product of the human mind, they tend to think of arithmetic, algebra, and geometry as having been completely explored in some never-never land of the past. True, they have heard vaguely of the existence of mathematicians like Euclid and Newton. But most people are inclined to believe that all numbers, all computational processes, and all geometric figures were invented by the ancients. It comes as a surprise therefore to be told that mathematics is a dynamic, exploding field of knowledge, even as science, art, and history are. Is not $2 + 2 = 4$ a fact that is still true? Of course it is. But today there are new ideas about numbers, new ways of performing computations, new theorems that are being proved in geometry, and completely new fields of mathematics. Mathematics, in short, is a continually developing field whose developments extend to our own day. In fact, it has been claimed that more important ideas in mathematics have been developed in the past hundred and fifty years than in all of mankind's previous history. To mention just a few and their inventors:

1. The development of non-Euclidean geometry by such men as the Hungarian John Bolyai, the Russian Nikolai Lobachevsky, and the German Georg Riemann.
2. The development of the theory of sets, starting with the German mathematician Georg Cantor.
3. The "cleaning up" of the assumptions of Euclidean mathematics by David Hilbert, also a German mathematician.
4. The invention of the branch of mathematics known as "game theory" by John von Neumann, a brilliant mathematician who was born in Germany but who spent his last days as a colleague of Einstein at the Institute for Advanced Study at Princeton.

1

5. The development of the modern electronic computer and the science of computer programming, which is based on the symbolic logic of George Boole, an Englishman.

Until recently, the elementary and high-school mathematics curriculums were singularly immune from virtually all of these new developments. As John Kemeny, chairman of the department of mathematics at Dartmouth, has pointed out, until recently mathematics has been "the only school subject you can study for fourteen years [through sophomore calculus] without learning anything that's been done since the year 1800."

But, one may justifiably ask, is this necessarily bad? Must one teach something new simply because of its newness? Unfortunately some enthusiasts for modern mathematics have given the impression that it is the novelty, the up-to-dateness of the changed curriculum which is its chief virtue. If this were true in other fields, such as literature, for example, we would abandon the study of Shakespeare, Milton, and Swift, in favor of Hemingway, Faulkner, and Allen Ginsberg.

What is valuable about the new mathematics is not that it is new but rather that it offers an opportunity to learn mathematics in a more meaningful way than had heretofore been possible. As we shall see in the course of this book, most of the mathematical ideas and skills which we were exposed to as students have not been discarded. Rather, they have been enriched by new insights. For example, the very concept of the troublesome x, the "unknown" (and, to too many students, the unknowable) in an algebraic equation, takes on new meaning. Such a basic idea in mathematics as number is re-examined from a conceptual point of view and takes on new significance. The common arithmetic operations—addition, subtraction, multiplication, and division—are seen to have characteristics that make of them more than the simple mechanical operations that have bored countless generations of arithmetic students. Geometry, to so many students simply a rather arbitrary repetition of a series of proofs of the obvious, is given new depth and is placed in the mainstream of mathematics. New mathematics, then, is meaningful mathematics—meaningful both to the mathematician and, if well taught, to the young student.

One of the most startling new factors in our "mathematized" society is the computer. The modern high-speed computer is creating a revolution that is perhaps even greater than the industrial revolution. The computer controls space ships, nuclear devices, automated factories, and political strategy. Who should be teaching this new computer science?

The computer is related to the new school mathematics in several ways. Many of the new topics in the new programs such as numeration systems, sets, and symbolic logic are used in programming the computer. Computer programming may also be an effective way of learning mathematical ideas. New programs are debating whether or not mathematics courses should include computer programming and whether or not high-school mathematics departments should have a computer as one of their necessary pieces of equipment.

The new uses of mathematics in our culture have major implications for the school program. We must teach more mathematics to more students. We must prepare our children with ideas and skills so that they will be able to use their knowledge in solving the problems of the future. We must develop the mathematical potential of our children so that they can pursue the many important careers that are dependent on a mathematical background. We must give them an adequate background of mathematical knowledge so that they will understand our democratic society and the world of nature in which we live.

Today there are new applications of mathematics which were never dreamed of a few years ago. Scientists are using new fields of mathematics to fill in gaps in knowledge of chemistry, physics, biology, and electronics. Psychologists are using mathematics to study human learning and behavior. Social scientists are using mathematics to study crime, economics, and politics. Even linguists are using mathematical analysis to study our language. And businessmen are using the mathematics of probability and linear programming to schedule production and distribution.

Another important reason for introducing a new school mathematics program is to improve the teaching of mathematics. We have new knowledge of how children learn. We know that complex ideas can be learned more effectively when children participate actively in the classroom activities. We know that children can learn complex ideas at a very young age. We have new teaching aids such as programmed texts, films, models, charts, pamphlets, books, and educational TV programs. The federal government, through the National Defense Education Act, has stimulated the development of new teaching aids and has given schools financial support for the purchase of these aids.

Thus, it now seems possible for a competent teacher with adequate teaching aids to teach mathematical ideas and skills much more efficiently than in the past.

Probably the greatest weakness of the traditional mathematics was the fact that thousands of students who were subjected to years of study of the subject came away from their courses with a certain degree of competence in skills, but with virtually no concept of what they were doing. Here, for example, is a list of questions relating to the "why" of certain simple arithmetic operations. If you can answer more than half of them, you had either extraordinary teachers or an unusual insight into the processes:*

1. When you divide one fraction by another ($\frac{1}{2} \div \frac{1}{4}$, for example) why do you invert the divisor ($\frac{1}{4}$) and multiply?

2. When you do the subtraction

$$\begin{array}{r} 37 \\ -\ 9 \\ \hline \end{array}$$

    what do you do that makes it possible for you to subtract the 9 from the 7?

3. In this multiplication

$$\begin{array}{r} 43 \\ \times 67 \\ \hline 301 \\ 258 \\ \hline 2881 \end{array}$$

    why do you write the 8 of 258 under the 0 of 301, rather than under the 1?

4. In dividing 12 by 0.2, why is the answer 60 rather than 6 or 600?

5. If division is a process that breaks something into smaller parts, why, when you divide $\frac{1}{4}$ by $\frac{1}{8}$ is the answer, 2, larger than either $\frac{1}{4}$ or $\frac{1}{8}$?

6. When you add $\frac{1}{6}$ and $\frac{1}{12}$, why must you first change $\frac{1}{6}$ to $\frac{2}{12}$?

* The answers to these questions will be found in Chapter 5 on pages 83–84.

7. You pay for a $0.65 luncheon check with a dollar bill. If subtraction means "take away," why does the cashier check her subtraction

$$\begin{array}{r} \$1.00 \\ -0.65 \end{array}$$

by *adding* like this: $0.65, $0.35, $1.00?

8. Why is the product of two negative numbers a positive number, for example, $^-3 \times {}^-5 = {}^+15$?

9. In dividing 7.68 by 4.2, why do you "move" the decimal point in the computation?

$$4.2\,\overline{)7.68} \rightarrow 42.\,\overline{)76.8}$$

10. How do we know that $\frac{3}{4} = 75/100$?

When mathematics is looked upon merely as a tool, a collection of facts and skills, teaching it consists largely of drills and mechanics, memorizations and manipulations. Then mathematics becomes a grind, a distasteful activity lacking intellectual flavor. This should never be the case because mathematics is one of the greatest creations of the human mind. There should be satisfaction in the study of mathematics similar to the enjoyment of literature, history, music, science, or art. In the outmoded classroom, the mathematics textbook or workbook is followed slavishly. The students work endless sets of drill exercises, memorize rules, and write out proofs of theorems so that their responses are largely automatic, like those of trained horses at the circus. The students can perform long division, factor involved expressions, draw graphs of equations, but rarely can they explain the process involved. Mathematics for them consists of a series of tricks to be performed only when required. No wonder the students lose interest in mathematics when they are taught in this fashion.

Dissatisfaction with this state of affairs is not of recent origin. Mathematics educators have been attempting for many years to improve the teaching of elementary and high school mathematics. One group of educators felt that if students could be made to see how useful mathematics is as a tool in everyday life, they would increase their interest, and consequently their skill in mathematics. This "social utility" school of mathematics education was an improvement over what had gone on before. But in stressing social utility, this school taught mathematics that was lacking in structure and organization. In short, it undersold mathematics itself.

Later, mathematics educators agreed that real progress could be made if the mathematics to which students were exposed could be made meaningful to them. They believed that students should know the "why" of arithmetic as well as the "how." They felt that students could be made to see what lies behind the mystery of such topics as long division, operations with fractions, decimals, and percentage—topics which are high on the list of disliked subjects of both students and teachers. This movement to stress the meaning of arithmetic began shortly after World War II and quickened pace in the early 1950's. Many new textbooks were written from this point of view, and considerable progress in improving the teaching of mathematics was made.

But these mathematics reformers were operating within the rather narrow framework of traditional mathematical subject matter. They ignored the many changes that had been taking place in the body of mathematics itself. If they were aware of the changes at all, they usually dismissed them as being unsuited to the elementary and high-school mathematics curriculum.

In the mid-1950's new voices began to be heard in school mathematics. Many came from people who were distressed at the fact that much of the mathematics being taught in the schools was old mathematics, that much that had been discovered in mathematics in the past hundred and fifty years could be profitably brought into the schools. They felt, too, that mathematics was proving distasteful to students because it presented no intellectual challenge; it was dull and drab. The insights provided by new developments in mathematics could do much to stimulate the student to think creatively in mathematics.

Part of the trouble with school mathematics, too, the new critics believed, was that mathematics was a coat of too many colors. It had little or no unity. One topic seemed to have little or no relationship to other topics. Mathematics, they felt strongly, should be presented as a many-sided, yet unified discipline. With the traditional content it was almost impossible to do this. The new content provided the means to deal with mathematics as a unified whole.

Teaching procedures also came under criticism. Even with the recent development of the emphasis on meaning, much teaching of mathematics was routine. The teacher handed out rules and precepts and the student's job was to act as a super-sponge. On one day he was expected to absorb the teacher's words and on the next, after the proper amount of practice, done as homework, he was wrung dry by class recitation and examination. A new breed of mathematics educator, appalled at these unimaginative procedures, called for a kind of instruction in which the student would be permitted to participate in the discovery of mathematical ideas. This kind of educator believed the teacher should serve as a guide and motivator, making it possible for the student to gain meaningful insights into the subject.

The case made against traditional mathematics education was an effective one. Energetic and imaginative men and women, about whom we shall have more to say in a later chapter, set to work and within an amazingly short time created new curriculums in high-school and elementary-school mathematics. Let us now describe in a general way the nature of the new curriculums.

Today our schools have a new mathematics model on display. Mathematics has a new look—the content, vocabulary, and presentation have changed. This new model is as different from the traditional program as the latest model automobile is different from the Model T Ford. But just as new automobile models use the same basic parts—engine, frame, and body—so school mathematics still consists largely of arithmetic, algebra, and geometry. However, the new model is far superior in comfort, power, and appearance to the traditional model. The new mathematics is more comfortable because it emphasizes understanding, more powerful because it is built on the logical structure of mathematics, more beautiful because of new vocabulary, new topics, and new presentation of old ideas.

To parents the most obvious changes in school mathematics are the new topics. As parents we have probably heard most about such new mathematical topics as sets and binary numerals. But in addition there is a host of other new topics such as probability, inequalities, finite number systems, and symbolic logic. These are the topics mathematicians feel are essential for understanding mathematics and for applying mathematics to modern science. These are the topics that students and teachers have found enhance the study of mathematics. We will explore some of them in later chapters.

We have said that the new mathematics attempts to present mathematics as a unified discipline. The study of sets is a good illustration of how new ideas are used to unify mathematical concepts. Sets are used to give meaning to the idea of a number. They are used to explain the meaning of addition and subtraction, to illustrate fractions and decimals, and to describe geometric figures. Graphs are discussed as sets of points, and the solutions of equations are described as truth sets. Sets are used to explain probability as well as to give meaning to measurements, and they are used to illustrate the logic of mathematics.

However, let us repeat that the "old" mathematics has not been discarded. Whole numbers, fractions, decimals, and percents are still being studied. Measurement, graphing, equations, and geometry are still in the curriculum. Development of skill in computation, problem solving, and proving theorems is receiving as much attention as before.

To make room for new topics, the treatment of some old topics has been radically changed. The number of drill problems in arithmetic and algebra has been drastically reduced. The modern point of view is that computational skill is best developed through problem solving, application, discovery, and thorough understanding of the computational process.

More time for studying new topics has been attained by cutting down on the applications of mathematics in business, home, and government. Topics such as banking, budgets, stocks and bonds, installment buying, taxation, and insurance are no longer considered suitable content for mathematics. These social applications have been eliminated for several reasons. They merely require computation, usually with percents and decimals. These are best dealt with in connection with fractions and ratios, without involving the social situation. And the social aspects of these topics can better be treated in social science or business courses— or perhaps by parents. Furthermore, in these changing times, when computing machines are performing many routine mathematical computations, the applications of today may be unimportant in the future. The object of the new mathematics is to give the student a sound understanding of basic principles so he can make whatever applications are called for in the future.

The new topics have resulted in essentially new courses at the secondary level. Seventh- and eighth-grade mathematics is now largely the study of sets, measurement, algebra, and geometry. Ninth-grade algebra is largely the study of the properties of number systems. Tenth-grade mathematics is still geometry but this includes plane geometry, solid geometry, and coordinate geometry. Eleventh-grade algebra stresses functions and the real and complex number systems. Twelfth-grade mathematics may include semesters of matrix algebra, polynomial functions, or probability rather than the traditional solid geometry and trigonometry.

The new courses, in addition to teaching new content, have been introducing mathematical ideas much earlier than traditional programs did. Experimental projects have found that children can learn many ideas at a much younger age than we had previously suspected. For example, Patrick Suppes of Stanford University has found that first graders can perform the geometric constructions that are usually taught in tenth-grade geometry. He has found that sixth graders can learn the symbolic logic which he usually teaches in his college logic course. Robert Davis of Webster College in Webster Groves, Missouri, has been able to teach fifth graders how to solve quadratic equations, a topic usually taught in eleventh-grade mathematics. As a result, a group of mathematicians and educators, who met in conference in Cambridge, Massachusetts, in 1963, has predicted that in a generation or less we will be able to compress our mathematics courses so that the mathematics now completed after three years in college will be completed in high school. Paul C. Rosenbloom, formerly of Minnesota, now at Columbia University, agrees that this will be possible, and, to hasten the process, he is developing materials for parents to use for preschool mathematical experiences with their children.

This earlier introduction of ideas is emphasized in many new programs. Professor Rosenbloom's Minnemath Project is presenting the number line, including positive and negative numbers, in the primary grades. The School Mathematics Study Group's elementary school program includes in grades 4–6 many ideas from algebra and geometry. The new textbooks at the elementary and junior high school levels are introducing many of the traditional topics two or three years earlier than formerly. Already modern senior high school texts are including many of the ideas of traditional college algebra and analytic geometry courses.

This earlier introduction of topics should come as no surprise. It has been a process that has been going on for centuries. When Columbus discovered America, students did not study long division until in the university. The college mathematics of 150 years ago was largely today's high-school mathematics.

Another hallmark of the new programs is the use of new words and new symbols. In discussing computation, terms such as "distributive principle," "identity element," "closure," and "inverse operation" are used. In algebra we find new expressions such as "truth set," "additive inverse," and "ordered pair." Similarly we find new symbols such as $\cup$, $\cap$, $>$, $\rightarrow$, and $\nless$. It is not the purpose of these terms to frustrate parents or confuse pupils. Rather it is the intent to add precision and understanding to mathematical operations.

One of the most common illustrations of the new precision in language is the difference between "number" and "numeral." A number is an idea. A numeral is a symbol. Thus the symbol "4" or the word "four" are numerals for the number 4 just as "John" is the name of a boy, and not the boy himself. Hence, there are many other numerals for 4, such as IV, $3 + 1$, 2×2, $\frac{12}{3}$, $\sqrt{16}$, and $9 - 5$. Why is this distinction helpful? This can be illustrated by an addition using fractions:

$$\frac{3}{4} + \frac{2}{3} = \, ?$$

$$\frac{3}{4} = \frac{9}{12}, \qquad \frac{2}{3} = \frac{8}{12}$$

$$\frac{9}{12} + \frac{8}{12} = \frac{17}{12} = 1\frac{5}{12}$$

In performing this addition we are merely writing new numerals for $\frac{3}{4}$, $\frac{2}{3}$, and $\frac{17}{12}$.

Another hallmark of modern mathematics is the emphasis on the "why" of mathematical operations. Too often in the past we have performed computations by "moving the decimal point" or "inverting the fraction" or "borrowing one." To avoid tricks, half-truths, and meaningless manipulations, the new programs emphasize the meaning of numerals and the basis for computation.

When we "borrow one" to subtract $32 - 7$ we regroup so that we are really subtracting 7 from 12 in this fashion: $32 - 7 = 20 + (12 - 7) = 20 + 5 = 25$. When we change $(2.87 \div 1.4)$ to $(28.7 \div 14)$ we are saying that

$$\frac{2.87}{1.4} = \frac{2.87}{1.4} \times 1 = \frac{2.87}{1.4} \times \frac{10}{10} = \frac{28.7}{14}$$

This emphasis on the "why" of mathematics should remove much of the mystery of mathematics. When a person knows why a process works, he should be able to apply it to a variety of new situations. And he should remember it longer.

In learning the why of computations, the pupil learns some basic laws which are used throughout mathematics. For example, the properties of 1, which tell us that $8 \times 1 = 8$ and $8 \div 8 = 1$, are useful in advanced mathematics. The basic principle illustrated by $3 \times 4 = 4 \times 3$, and called the *commutative property*, is a big idea in algebra and number theory. These basic principles learned in the early years permit a more logical development of mathematics throughout the grades.

We have mentioned that many of the reformers have been as concerned with *how* mathematics ought to be taught as with *what* might be taught. They realized that a renovation in the curriculum could not suffice if the methods used in teaching that curriculum were deficient. No curriculum, no matter how modern, how advanced, teaches itself. If a teacher does not teach traditional mathematics in an exciting, challenging way, why should one assume that he will teach the new curriculum any more effectively? A new curriculum is no substitute for improved teaching.

The new programs have explored a new approach to the teaching of mathematics—one that would motivate students to learn, that would encourage students to discuss mathematical ideas. This general method has been given the name of "discovery" teaching. In this type of teaching the pupils are expected to discover ideas for themselves. They are not told answers as part of the normal teaching process. More questions are likely to be asked by a teacher than answered in a good discovery lesson. Broadly speaking, this method is based on the premise that we learn through experiences rather than through memorization. Discovery takes place through experiments, thinking, discussion, the study of patterns. When a student discovers new ideas, he gains insight, confidence, and interest in learning. Later we will present a sample lesson using the discovery method.

Another point of emphasis in the new courses is the structure of mathematics. Mathematics is an organized body of knowledge that is based on a relatively small set of principles and operations. An example is the commutative property for addition, $2 + 5 = 5 + 2$. Mathematics is also the science of logical deductions. Every mathematical statement can be proved by a sequence of steps or arguments. Each topic or field of mathematics is a logical structure. The basic parts of this structure are assumptions, definitions, and theorems like those you learned in geometry. When you understand the pattern of this structure, and how the ideas involved are related, you have a sense of mastery of mathematics. Then mathematics makes sense, you appreciate the elegance of mathematics, and you understand the power of mathematics. This power resides in the abstractness of mathematics rather than in its computational aspect.

This emphasis on structure is also in agreement with current principles of learning. Psychologists are saying that we learn a subject best when we see its structure. When you have a complete picture of the organization of a topic, you will remember this topic, and you will be able to apply your knowledge to a new situation. Since we do not know what the mathematics of the future will be, understanding the structure of the subject appears to be the most appropriate foundation for continued study and use of the mathematics of today.

However, it is the new spirit of mathematics that is the most exciting aspect of the new programs. Mathematics is presented as a field of human invention which is worthy of study by itself. New courses talk about mathematics, its organization, its unity, its power. Mathematics is discussed as a field to be considered for a profession, and the study of mathematics is enriched by readings on the history of mathematics, biographies of mathematicians, and exciting mathematical diversions. For youngsters, learning mathematics in this setting should be an exciting adventure rather than a source of frustration.

HOW THE NEW MATHEMATICS PROGRAMS DEVELOPED

2

The new school mathematics programs illustrate the remarkable progress that can be made when imaginative people work together and have adequate financial support. Most of the experimental projects in mathematics have been the cooperative efforts of mathematicians, educators, and schoolteachers. These groups have been established by professional organizations or universities. They have been supported by private foundations or government funds.

Materials have been produced by some of these groups at a phenomenal rate. For example, the School Mathematics Study Group was organized in March 1958. By September of the same year they had experimental texts ready for the secondary school. Now the many publications of this group fill many feet of bookshelf space.

Participation in these new programs was a tremendously stimulating experience for teachers and students. Their enthusiasm was contagious and encouraged many schools to participate.

Actually there have been committees and commissions recommending changes in school mathematics since the 1890's. Some of the proposals of the early 1900's, such as discovery teaching, have been echoed by the reform groups of the past 10 years.

Who are the people and the organizations involved in the new programs of the current generation? Let's consider the most significant ones in chronological order, according to their time of organization.

UNIVERSITY OF ILLINOIS COMMITTEE ON SCHOOL MATHEMATICS (UICSM)

The first group to prepare a new mathematics program was organized at the University of Illinois in 1952. The personnel of this group has included professors of mathematics, education, and engineering, and high school teachers. The director is Max Beberman, a high-school mathematics teacher and professor of education at the University.

Dr. Beberman is noted for his remarkable skill as a teacher and for his creative ideas. His demonstration lessons at the University of Illinois High School and at conferences have been an inspiration for many teachers. He has always been of the opinion that the success of any mathematics course depends more on the teacher than on the text material. The films of his lessons teaching the Illinois material are dramatic illustrations of how to use the discovery approach.

Dr. Beberman is untiring in sharing his ideas with fellow teachers. He is courageous in presenting a point of view which may be at variance with the views of other scholars. At the same time, he is ready to discard an idea when it is found to be indefensible. This quality has added to the great influence he has had in promoting the Illinois mathematics program. Presently Dr. Beberman is concerned that new programs may have been accepted by schools before the teachers are ready to teach them.

The Illinois Project was first supported by grants from the Carnegie Corporation and later by the Federal government through National Science Foundation grants. Experimental texts with teachers' editions were developed for grades nine through twelve. These texts received extensive tryouts in schools throughout the country and were frequently revised as a result. Until 1958 the texts were available only to those teachers who had received special training in their use. Even now the group advocates the use of the texts only by those who receive instruction or supervision in their use. The teachers' commentaries are most extensive in suggesting how to present the material, since they are based on many years of experimentation.

The experimental texts include most of traditional high-school mathematics. However, many new topics are included, and new approaches, new symbolism, new problems, and new vocabulary are introduced. The Illinois texts are also unique in their use of the discovery approach, in the sequence of the topics, and in their careful treatment of logic and proof. Rules are not stated as such but are meant to be discovered by the students in their independent solution of a series of problems.

The major points of emphasis of the Illinois program are the following:

1. Only mathematics that is correct and based on a logical structure should be presented.

2. The success of a new program depends on good teaching by teachers well grounded in mathematics.
3. The language and symbolism used should make the presentation precise.

While the Illinois program, in common with other modern programs, is concerned with the logical structure of mathematics, it assumes that mathematical knowledge is not always acquired in a logical fashion—nor, the Illinois educators say, should it be. They place great emphasis on the intuitive aspect of learning. They are not concerned if a student is unable to state a principle in words; it is more important to them for him to demonstrate his understanding of the principle by being able to work with it.

A unique invention of the UICSM is the term *pronumeral* as an analog of the grammatical term *pronoun*. In the sentence, "He is late," the word *he* is a pronoun that stands for a noun, the name of some person. If we knew his name we could substitute it for *he*, as in, "George is late."

In mathematics we also have sentences, but they take the form of

$$\square + 9 = 12$$

or

$$x + 9 = 12$$

Here the $\square$ and x are serving a function similar to *he* in the English sentence: they are pronumerals that stand for a numeral. If we replace $\square$ and x with the numeral 3, our statement

$$3 + 9 = 12$$

will be a true statement.

Ingenious tests have been devised to evaluate the achievement of students studying the Illinois texts. The teachers and students who use these texts are enthusiastic about them even though the level of abstraction and rigor would indicate that they are most appropriate for above-average students.

The Illinois Committee has recently received financial support from the National Science Foundation to extend its program to grades seven and eight and to write new materials for the secondary school. The experimental texts for grades nine through twelve are now available from the D. C. Heath Company, Boston, Massachusetts.

COMMISSION ON MATHEMATICS OF THE COLLEGE ENTRANCE
EXAMINATION BOARD

The College Entrance Examination Board appointed a Commission
on Mathematics in 1955 for the purpose of improving the program of
college preparatory mathematics in the secondary schools. The commission, supported by funds from the Carnegie Corporation, consisted
of mathematicians and high school mathematics teachers, with
Albert E. Meder of Rutgers University as executive director.

The commission reported its findings in 1958. It proposed that every
student should have a challenging and rewarding intellectual experience
studying the mathematical ideas and concepts that are needed for
everyday living as well as preparation for college. Also recommended
was the idea that the school mathematics curriculum be reshaped to
bring it into harmony with the methods and spirit of modern mathematics.

The commission outlined in detail the topics which it considered
essential for grades nine through twelve. The outline included most
of the classical mathematics of traditional courses but went far beyond
traditional content. The outline included new topics such as sets,
statistics, inequalities, probability, fields, and circular functions. In
addition, it recommended stress on understanding the nature and role
of deductive reasoning—in algebra, as well as in geometry—appreciation of mathematical structure—for example, properties of natural,
rational, real, and complex numbers, and the incorporation with plane
geometry of some coordinate geometry, and essentials of solid geometry and space perception, as well as certain other changes, in the
courses for the eleventh and twelfth grades.

Although the commission did not publish experimental texts, the
appendix of its report included sample units to illustrate the new language, symbolism, content, and emphasis. Since the report of the
commission has been used extensively by experimental projects and
textbook writers, it has been a major influence in the revision of the
high-school curriculum.

UNIVERSITY OF MARYLAND MATHEMATICS PROJECT (UMMaP)

This project was the first to devote itself to the improvement
of seventh- and eighth-grade mathematics. It began in 1957 and
involved the preparation and use of experimental texts for these
grades. Beginning in 1960 this group prepared materials in mathe-

matics for elementary school teachers and conducted studies in the learning of mathematics. The personnel of UMMaP includes professors of mathematics, education, psychology and engineering, public school supervisors of mathematics, classroom teachers, administrators, and government specialists in mathematics education. The project was financed by grants from the Carnegie Corporation. The director is John R. Mayor, professor of mathematics at the University of Maryland and director of education for the American Association for the Advancement of Science. Dr. Mayor has taught mathematics in high school and college and methods of teaching mathematics.

The active participation of Dr. Mayor in the many professional organizations and his varied publications have been highly influential in mathematics education. His congenial spirit, his dry humor, and his keen insight have contributed much to building a cooperative spirit between mathematicians and educators. His experiences in a variety of classrooms have given him an understanding of learning problems that has been invaluable in his direction of educational projects.

The experimental texts and accompanying teachers' manuals of this project have been used in classrooms throughout the United States. The texts introduce a variety of new topics such as sets, logic, statistics, probability, irrational numbers, and numerical trigonometry, equations, and algebraic expressions. Much of the traditional content of seventh- and eighth-grade mathematics courses is also a part of Maryland courses but the topics are approached from a new point of view. Precise language and mathematical structure are stressed. This group believes that computational skill is still of major importance but that this skill is best attained by emphasis on mathematical concepts, language, and structure. These courses are now available from Holt, Rinehart & Winston, Inc., New York, N.Y.

The Maryland material has been evaluated by a one-year study of each course. The results of this evaluation indicate that students in the new courses did as well as students studying traditional courses. In addition, students in the new courses learned a great number of new ideas beyond those of a traditional course.

SCHOOL MATHEMATICS STUDY GROUP (SMSG)

The School Mathematics Study Group, SMSG for short, has probably had more influence on the secondary mathematics curriculum than any other experimental group, largely through the extensive use of its many textbooks. It is estimated that over 10 percent of our secondary school mathematics students use SMSG textbooks. SMSG was organized in 1958 by the American Mathematical Society, the National Council of Teachers of Mathematics, and the Mathematical Association of America, with funds supplied by the National Science Foundation. The group consists of mathematicians, mathematics teachers, educators, psychologists, and representatives from science and technology. Its immediate purpose was to prepare textbooks for high schools along modern lines. This it did with dispatch. During the summer of 1958, just a few months following its organization, writing teams based at Yale University, operating on a crash schedule, were able to produce texts in time for use in experimental classrooms in the school year 1958–59. Additional texts were produced the following summer, revised in 1960, and all texts were made available for general use by the school public in the same year.

Directing this feverish activity was the head of SMSG, Edward G. Begle, professor of mathematics at Yale when SMSG was founded, but now professor of mathematics education at Stanford University. Dr. Begle outwardly is a quiet, retiring college professor, but he has proved himself to be a fine administrator and an enthusiastic publicist for the work of his organization. He is an untiring worker and sets the tone for the continuing work of the writing teams of the SMSG project.

After its texts for high schools were written, SMSG turned its attention to the elementary schools. It now has text materials for grades 1 through 12. It also has programmed texts for the ninth grade. Enrichment materials for superior students and background materials for mathematics teachers have been prepared in separate pamphlets and books. All materials except the enrichment booklets may be purchased from Yale University Press, New Haven, Connecticut. The enrichment booklets are available from Random House, New York, New York.

The basic philosophy of SMSG is the following:

1. Basic mathematical concepts should be introduced at a much earlier age than has been done in the past.
2. The language of mathematics should be precise.
3. The deductive structure of mathematics should be introduced at least in the junior high school years and should be stressed in all courses.
4. Mathematical ideas should be presented in interesting narrative and through discovery activities.

5. Mathematics courses should teach the role of mathematics in society but specific applications of mathematics are of minor importance.
6. The mathematics courses developed are for the college-capable student.

The SMSG text materials have been subjected to rigorous evaluation in a variety of research studies. In general, these studies show that the students in SMSG courses do as well in traditional concepts and skills as the students from traditional courses. However, it is reasonable to assume that the student of the SMSG courses has learned many new ideas and skills not covered by texts based on traditional mathematics.

The major changes which have been incorporated in the SMSG program are the following:

1. At the elementary level new topics are introduced such as sets, numeration systems, the properties of numbers, the number line, equations, and geometric concepts.
2. In the seventh and eighth grades new topics such as non-metric geometry, probability, proof, statistics, mathematical systems, factoring and primes, and measurement, replace the traditional applications of arithmetic to banking, taxation, installment buying, and investment.
3. In the ninth grade the SMSG course is largely algebra with emphasis on number properties, elementary proofs, the number line for real numbers, graphs, and sentences. These sentences include inequalities as well as equalities. The mechanical manipulation of algebraic expressions in factoring and in equations is reduced in emphasis.
4. In the tenth grade the geometry course includes concepts from solid geometry and coordinate geometry as well as the traditional concepts and proofs of plane geometry.
5. In the eleventh grade the SMSG text includes the usual topics of intermediate high school algebra and trigonometry texts. In addition there is extensive material on the real number system, the complex numbers, vector algebra, algebraic structures, and analytic geometry.
6. In the twelfth grade the course involves functions, matrices, and vectors.

It was to be expected that a program as extensive in scope and as extensively used would be subjected to energetic criticism. The most widely heard objections to the SMSG courses are these:

1. The applications of mathematics are largely ignored.
2. The rigor and symbolism are too great for even a large portion of the college-capable school population.
3. The content outlined for each grade is too extensive to be adequately presented in the time available.
4. The time devoted to the practice of computational skills is inadequate.

Whatever the validity of these criticisms, we must recognize that the SMSG has been a tremendous stimulant to the improvement of mathematics instruction in the schools not only of the United States but of Europe as well.

GREATER CLEVELAND MATHEMATICS PROGRAM (GCMP)

The Greater Cleveland Mathematics Program is a product of the Educational Research Council of Greater Cleveland, an organization dedicated to curriculum improvement in a number of fields. The GCMP was started in 1959 with the purpose of developing a new mathematics program for all children from kindergarten through grade twelve. The primary emphasis is placed upon thinking, reasoning, and understanding rather than on purely mechanical responses to standard situations. The child is encouraged to investigate new ideas, to make generalizations, and to find new applications.

The elementary school course includes much traditional content but it is presented at an earlier age. In addition, the presentation involves new symbolism, new emphasis on number properties and computational properties, and unusual problem situations. These problem situations involve the discovery of new ideas as well as the applications of ideas already learned. Teachers' guides are available to give the teacher the necessary mathematical background and to suggest developmental teaching procedures. A series of teacher-training films on both content and method have been produced. The texts are now available from Science Reasearch Associates, Chicago, Illinois.

The guidelines for this program are:

1. The basic program must be suitable for *all* students.
2. The program must have a continuous sequence of mathematical concepts from kindergarten through grade twelve.

3. The presentation of the material should use the discovery method of teaching whenever possible.
4. The material should be challenging and interesting to the student.
5. The program must be mathematically correct and pedagogically sound.

The text materials of this project are being tried out in classrooms and revised on the basis of teacher recommendations. In standardized tests, children using the experimental texts for one year scored higher on computation and problem solving than children of similar age and ability using conventional texts. The subjective evaluation of teachers using this material indicates enthusiastic acceptance by teachers and children.

COMMITTEE ON THE UNDERGRADUATE PROGRAM IN MATHEMATICS (CUPM)

In 1959 the Mathematical Association of America selected a Committee on the Undergraduate Program in Mathematics to make recommendations for the improvement of college mathematics. This committee selected teams of mathematicians to prepare course outlines. It is expected that these outlines will be used by independent authors in preparing commercial textbooks.

The committee is supported financially by the Ford Foundation and the National Science Foundation. Emphasis has been placed on preparing mathematics courses for elementary teachers and secondary mathematics teachers. In addition this committee has prepared new programs designed for the mathematics preparation of engineers, physical scientists, and social scientists. This committee is the major group influencing the modernization of college mathematics.

COMMITTEE ON MATHEMATICS FOR THE NON-COLLEGE BOUND

The Committee on Mathematics for the Non-College Bound was appointed by and supported financially by the National Council of Teachers of Mathematics in 1963. It was the purpose of this committee to produce text material for students who do not plan to attend college. This committee has produced an experimental text for ninth grade, *Experiences in Mathematical Discovery*, which is a radical departure from the typical ninth-grade general mathematics text. Topics included in this text are patterns, formulas, graphs, permutations and combinations, probability, intuitive geometry, ratio and proportion, directed numbers, measurement, fractions, and deduction. Conspicuous by their absence are topics such as banking, installment buying, stocks and bonds, and taxation, which were traditional in general mathematics courses. This is the only experimental project devoted to improving mathematics for the slow learners. If it is successful it will undoubtedly encourage many schools to use the new mathematics in courses for the slow learner.

MINNESOTA SCHOOL MATHEMATICS CENTER (MINNEMATH)

A center for the development of new curricula in mathematics was organized at the University of Minnesota in 1958. This center was established by Paul C. Rosenbloom and is supported by National Science Foundation funds. It is currently involved in writing an integrated mathematics and science curriculum for kindergarten through grade nine. This center is also testing experimentally an integrated science-mathematics course at the twelfth-grade level related to computer programming. Other activities of this center involve the preparation of films and correspondence courses for mathematics teachers. Professor Rosenbloom is an imaginative and creative scholar. His depth of knowledge in mathematics and science and his skill in writing material which ranges from the kindergarten to the graduate level are an indication of his ingenuity.

OTHER EXPERIMENTAL PROJECTS

There is a variety of other projects in elementary and secondary mathematics that are more limited in scope than the major ones discussed above. We list the major ones here:

1. *Syracuse University-Webster College Madison Project*, directed by Robert B. Davis. This project is producing a supplementary program of advanced topics for the elementary grades.
2. *Boston College Mathematics Institute*, directed by Stanley J. Bezuska. The experimental course, *Sets, Operations, and Patterns*, intended for the ninth grade, was written by Reverend Bezuska.
3. *Suppes Arithmetic Project*, directed by Patrick Suppes at Stanford University. This project has produced a series of workbooks for elementary school and is conducting research in learning mathematics.

When we compare the experimental programs of the groups described above, we find that they are similar in many ways. They are usually in agreement about the new topics to be introduced, the earlier introduction of traditional topics, the emphasis on structure and logic, the precision of language, and the use of the discovery method. However, they do not agree on the specific sequence of topics, the role of applications, or the role of computer science. They vary considerably in specific course recommendations for twelfth grade; some favor probability and statistics, others advocate college calculus. But they all agree that school mathematics needs new treatment from kindergarten through grade 12.

Much of the text material of the reform groups is now available for purchase. Most of the new mathematics textbooks produced by commercial publishers have incorporated their recommendations for content and sequence. However, most of the reform groups are still working on new programs. This suggests that school mathematics is likely to be in a state of flux for many years to come. That which is new mathematics today may well be out of date in the not-too-distant future.

MODERN TEACHING FOR MODERN MATHEMATICS

3

When the curriculum reformers assessed the task of improving school mathematics, the more astute among them realized the need not only for better content but for improved instruction as well. These men and women recognized that the new content would not teach itself. They knew that the new topics could become as drab as the traditional topics if taught by unenthusiastic, unimaginative, unskilled teachers. One group expressed it in these terms: "A poor curriculum well taught is better than a good curriculum poorly taught." The object of the reform groups is, of course, a good curriculum well taught.

This matter of improved teaching has several aspects because mathematics, with its abstract symbolism, its sequential organization, its logical structure, its wide application, has unique learning problems. At one extreme it involves simple memorizing of facts and practicing of skills. At the other extreme—solving a problem, proving a theorem, applying a generalization, building a mathematical structure—it requires a high level of creative thinking. Thus, the teacher of mathematics will need to know how to teach concepts, skills, proof, and productive thinking. The current emphasis on discovery, problem solving, and creative attitudes poses problems of adaptability and flexibility in the classroom that require far greater skill than the lecture-recitation style that has been typical of mathematics teaching in the past.

We have already noted that for the learning of mathematical ideas the new programs recommend the so-called discovery method. The discovery method is not a new idea. One of its first practitioners was Socrates; hence, it is sometimes called the Socratic method. Good teachers have been using this method for generations. But far too many teachers have failed to use it, either through ignorance or because it is a difficult method to master. It is not easy to master because it cannot be structured in advance. It must be adapted to the students involved, to their responses, questions, and experiences. It may turn up questions which the teacher cannot answer and ideas which are new to him. It is time consuming and patience trying. But the discovery method is the method of choice because understanding is more likely to result if the learner plays an active role in developing ideas.

The teacher wants mathematical ideas to have meaning to the learner. But he cannot "give" meaning to the learner. The learner creates his own meaning. And he creates this meaning on the basis of his perception of the situation. He relates the current idea to previous experiences, interests, emotions, memories, and ideas. Hence, it is the teacher's role to guide the learner to connect the new idea to his storehouse of knowledge and experiences.

When the learner discovers an idea which is new to him, he gets a sense of satisfaction, mastery, and confidence. This triumph of discovery nourishes curiosity for more learning. It is one of the best means of teaching how to learn independently. Discovery activities build initiative and self-reliance so that the learner can continue to explore new ideas in mathematics. Furthermore, discovery promotes a flexible, investigating, creative response to problems that is so essential for successful problem solving. It is this flexible approach that stimulates transfer and application to new situations.

How then does the teacher provide discovery experiences? First, the teacher plans a series of questions, problems, or laboratory exercises to present to the learners. The lesson begins with an introduction that gives the student a clear idea of what he is to explore.

After the teacher poses a problem, he stimulates the thinking of the students by a dialogue. Students are asked "Why is this correct?" rather than "What is correct?" Students are asked to explain "how" they arrived at an answer. Students are encouraged to comment on each others' answers. Students do not hesitate to state the results of their thinking for fear of being wrong or being embarrassed by the rejection of a poor suggestion. The skillful teacher will use half-formed ideas as stepping stones to a correct idea. Even a correct statement does not always mean that the student understands the idea. The teacher guides thinking by giving hints, relating the new idea to known ideas, requiring reasons for statements. He asks questions which force the student to test his answers, to find contradictions, to find special cases. He helps the student clarify a statement, locate an error, state a generalization. Thus, the dialogue is like a stairway in which one idea leads to another until the generalization is reached. It is the teacher's role to keep the investigation going at a challenging rate and in the proper direction. His role is not that of prosecuting attorney eliciting "yes" or "no" answers.

The best way to learn what is meant by discovery teaching is to sit in on a class session. Failing that, it would be enlightening to read a verbatim record of such a lesson. We present here a discovery lesson which took place in the seventh-grade class of William A. Harner, a teacher in the South Junior High School, Arlington Heights, Illinois.* It deals with a problem that seems to baffle most youngsters—division with fractions. Read it through and then try to compare it in your mind with the kind of instruction you received as a student of mathematics.

The teacher put this equation on the board. It resulted from the problem:
If $\frac{2}{3}$ of a pound of butter costs 46¢, what does one pound cost?

$$\frac{2}{3} \text{ of } N = 46 \left(\text{could be } \frac{2}{3} = \frac{46}{N} \right)$$

TEACHER: How would you find the value of N?
JIM K.:   What does N mean?
CAROL K.: N stands for a number.
JIM K.:   You mean $\frac{2}{3}$ of a number equals 46?
CAROL K.:   Yes.
TEACHER: From what is on the board, what do we know about the number N?
JIM K.:   If 46 is only $\frac{2}{3}$ of the number, then the number should be greater than 46.
TEACHER: How much greater?
            (no answer)
TEACHER: How can we find the value of N?
CHIP: Take any number and try $\frac{2}{3}$ of it.
TEACHER: What number would you like to try?
CHIP: Try 50.

$$\frac{2}{3} \text{ of } 50 = \frac{100}{3} = 33\frac{1}{3}$$

TEACHER: Would this be an acceptable answer?
CHIP: No.
TEACHER: Why not?
JIM K.:   Because it is not large enough.

* This lesson first appeared as an article by Mr. Harner entitled "The Problem in Seventh-Grade Mathematics," *The Mathematics Teacher* (November 1962), pp. 549–552. Reprinted with the kind permission of the editor of the journal.

TEACHER: Why?
BONNIE: Because $\frac{2}{3}$ of 50 does not equal 46.
CHIP: Okay. Then try 60.

$$\frac{2}{3} \text{ of } 60 \ = \ 40$$

BONNIE: Still not large enough.
RUSS: This is going to take a long time. There must be an easier way.
ED: If $\frac{2}{3}$ of N is equal to 46, you would need to find $\frac{1}{3}$ by dividing 46 by 3, and then multiply your answer by 3.
CAROL H.:   Don't be silly. If you divide 46 by 3, and then multiply by 3, you will still have 46.
ED: Well, how do you find $\frac{1}{3}$ of the number when $\frac{2}{3}$ of the number is 46?
JIM A.:   Why not divide 46 by $\frac{2}{3}$?
TEACHER: Write what you mean on the board.
JIM A.:   (at board)

$$\frac{2}{3} \div 46 \ = \ \frac{2}{3} \times \frac{1}{46} \ = \ \frac{1}{69}$$

JIM K.:   Won't work. $\frac{1}{69}$ is less than 46, and we have already agreed that N must be greater than 46.
JIM A.:   I mean $\frac{2}{3}$ of 46.
TEACHER: Try it on the board.
JIM A.:   (at board)

$$\frac{2}{3} \times 46 \ = \ \frac{92}{3} \ = \ 30\frac{1}{3}$$

ELLEN: That's no good either; still too small.
CHIP: Try 75.
TEACHER: Okay, try 75.
CHIP: (at board)

$$\frac{2}{3} \text{ of } 75 \ = \ 50$$

            That's better—now N is between 60 and 75.
RUSS: You are getting close, but your method is still too long.
TEACHER: Jim A., why did you divide $\frac{2}{3}$ by 46, or multiply 46 by $\frac{2}{3}$?
JIM A.:   You have only two numbers, so you must be able to do something with them. Addition doesn't make sense, neither does subtraction, so I tried division.
CAROL H.:   But your answer was wrong from both division and multiplication.
RUSS: You mean you can't do any of those?

BETH: We don't seem to be getting anywhere.
TEACHER: We have gone farther than you think.
             1. We know the number is between 60 and 75.
             2. We know the number is greater than 46.
             3. We know 46 is only part of the number N.
             4. We still are not sure of what arithmetic operation to use
                —perhaps Jim A. set the problem up wrong.
             Can someone see a different approach?
BETH: If $\frac{2}{3}$ of the number is 46, $\frac{1}{3}$ of the number must be 46 divided
             by 2. So add 23 to 46.
TEACHER: Put what you mean on the board.
BETH: (at board)

$$\frac{2}{3} \text{ of } N = 46$$

$$2\overline{)46}^{\,23} \qquad \begin{array}{r} 46 \\ +23 \\ \hline 69 \end{array}$$

             (No one made a remark at this time. The teacher made
             no effort to show what had happened mathematically.)
JOHN: It seems to me that if 46 is $\frac{2}{3}$ of the number, then $\frac{1}{3}$ of the
             number must be $\frac{1}{2}$ of 46, which is 23. The whole number
             must be three times as large, or 3×23, which is 69.
             (Again no comment from anyone about the result.
             Again the teacher actually played down possibility of
             remarks.)
JIM A.:   Now I know what I did wrong—I should have divided 46
             by $\frac{2}{3}$.
TEACHER: Would you like to try again?
             (said almost jokingly)
JIM A.:   Yes I would! (at board)

$$46 \div \frac{2}{3} = 46 \times \frac{3}{2} = 69$$

             There, I got the same number!
TEACHER: Anyone like to comment on what happened so far?
BONNIE: So far we have obtained the number 69 three times, so it
             must be the right answer.
CAROL K.:   Why did Jim A. divide by $\frac{2}{3}$?
JIM A.:   I just knew if I had two numbers I must be able to do
             something with them, so I tried division again and I was
             right.
TEACHER: How do we know that 69 is the correct answer?
BONNIE: We got it three times, it must be correct.
JIM K.:   It's greater than 46, and we got it three times.

CAROL H.: It is between 60 and 75, and Jim A. knows how to get the right answer.

TEACHER: But how can we really tell if 69 is the correct number?
(no comment from class)

CHIP: Try it in place of the N and see if it works.

TEACHER: Show us what you mean.

CHIP: (at board)

$$\frac{2}{3} \text{ of } 69 = 46$$

There, it works OK. 69 must be the correct number.

TEACHER: Many of you have been correct. You have tried trial and error, approximation, different computations, etc., but the important thing is that you tried something. That is better than doing nothing. You were helped by knowing that the number must be greater than 46. This alone was one clue worth a hundred methods of working the problem. You know about what your answer should be.

CAROL K.: But why did Jim A. divide by $\frac{2}{3}$ and get the right answer?

JIM A.: I knew I must do something to the two numbers.

RICKY: I know why. $\frac{2}{3}$ of N is like a multiplication problem: 46 is the product. If you have a product and one of the factors, you use the inverse operation (division) to find the other factor.

TEACHER: Very good. Do you understand what Ricky is talking about?

CAROL K.: No, I don't. "Of" means division, not multiplication.

JEANNE: "Of" means division, but you multiply to get your answer.

TEACHER: Can you give an example?

JEANNE: $\frac{1}{2}$ of $6 = 3$. You have to divide 6 into two parts and take one part. That's division. To get 3 through computation you use multiplication.

RICKY: When the 46 is the product and $\frac{2}{3}$ a factor of 46, you use division to find the other factor.

TEACHER: What Ricky has said is very true. This is one purpose of division, the inverse operation of multiplication. For example:

$$3 \times 6 = 18 \quad 3\overline{)18}^{\,6} \quad 6\overline{)18}^{\,3}$$

We had better summarize the facts you have given, and see what it all might look like in a mathematical form. Let's start with Beth's statement.

$$\frac{2}{3} \text{ of } N = 46 \tag{1}$$

$$\frac{1}{3} \text{ of } N = \frac{46}{2} = 23 \tag{2}$$

JOHN:

She said that 46 divided by 2 would give her $\frac{1}{3}$ of the N.
23 is $\frac{1}{3}$ of N. How can we find the whole amount?
One whole is equal to $\frac{3}{3}$, so multiply 23 by 3. Our number
is three times as large as 23.

$$\frac{3}{3} \text{ of } N = 3 \times 23 = 69 \qquad (3)$$

$$\therefore N = 69 \qquad (4)$$

TEACHER:

How do we know that 69 is correct?
(again no comment from group)

CHIP:

Put 69 in place of N.

$$\frac{2}{3} \text{ of } (69) = ? \qquad 46$$

$$46 = 46$$

CINDY: But why do you divide the 46 by 2 in the second step?

JOHN: So you can get $\frac{1}{3}$ of the number. If $\frac{2}{3}$ of the number is 46, then $\frac{1}{3}$ of the number must be $\frac{1}{2}$ as much.

CINDY: But why divide by 2 instead of taking $\frac{1}{2}$ of 46?

TEACHER: What times $\frac{1}{3}$ will give you $\frac{2}{3}$?

CINDY: 2 times $\frac{1}{3}$ will give $\frac{2}{3}$.

TEACHER: How can you go from $\frac{2}{3}$ to $\frac{1}{3}$?

CINDY: Divide by 2.

TEACHER: What is 46 in relation to the number N?

JEANNE: 46 is $\frac{2}{3}$ of the number.

TEACHER: How can you get from 46 which is $\frac{2}{3}$ of the number to $\frac{1}{3}$?

CINDY: Divide by 2. Oh! now I see.

TEACHER: Now let's look at the Jim A. method:

$$\frac{2}{3} \text{ of } N = 46$$

$$46 \div \frac{2}{3} = 46 \times \frac{3}{2} = 69$$

Once again, how can we check this result?

CHIP: Put it in the place of N.

CAROL K.:   Why does he divide by $\frac{2}{3}$?

BOB: It's the inverse operation. He is undoing his multiplication.

TEACHER: Let's try a few problems using one of the methods. The BJ (for Beth and John), or the JC (for Jim A. and Carol K.) method.

(Now out of a clear blue sky comes the remark that only a discussion period like the one mentioned above can lead to. The result of letting the young untracked mind wander and fall, and wander some more—creativity in mathematics.)

BOB: I was looking at the $46 \times \frac{3}{2}$ in the JC method—and was wondering if this would work. ... Why divide the 46 by the $\frac{2}{3}$? 46 is $\frac{2}{3}$ of the N. ∴ since $\frac{3}{2}$ is the reciprocal of $\frac{2}{3}$, the product of $\frac{2}{3}$ and its reciprocal is one or the whole thing: why not just multiply 46 which is $\frac{2}{3}$ by its reciprocal $\frac{3}{2}$ getting the whole which is 69?

$$\frac{3}{2} \times \frac{2}{3} = 1; \qquad \frac{3}{2} \times 46 = 69$$

You have probably noticed the important characteristics of this lesson. First, quite clearly, the atmosphere of the class was such that students did not hesitate to contribute to the discussion, even though they were not right all the time. Second, once the teacher triggered the discussion, he participated in it only at intervals—to summarize and occasionally to stimulate a certain line of thinking. Third, notice that the students were reacting to the comments of other students; they were not waiting for the teacher to hand them the solution to the problem. And, finally, the answer came from the students, as answers to other problems in this mathematics class must have come from the students.

Developing competence in computation has always been a major concern in mathematics. Skill in computation has been a goal for the superior student as well as for the slow learner. At the same time educators and parents have been and still are dissatisfied with the computational skill of youth in elementary school, in the high school, in college, and on the job. Their perennial complaint is "Our youngsters can't add, subtract, multiply, and divide." Psychologists and educators usually explain this lack of accomplishment upon factors such as lack of understanding of numbers and operations with numbers, lack of interest in attaining computational efficiency, lack of ability to cope with the abstract ideas and symbols of computation, and lack of effective teaching of computational processes. The new programs are trying to provide for each of these factors.

All of the new programs mentioned recognize that some kind of learning activity is necessary to build retention, accuracy, efficiency, and confidence in computational skills. In planning their drill activities good teachers take into account these principles of learning that are advocated by modern psychology:

1. The effectiveness of practice depends on the intent to improve. The learner must accept the goal of practice. He needs to be

aware of the advantages of attaining this goal and the handi-
caps that will result from failure to attain it.

2. Practice should be performed thoughtfully rather than
   mechanically. The learner should be able to justify the process,
   know the properties involved, or relate to the definition of
   the operation.

3. Practice should follow discovery and understanding. It is
   understanding which is the key to mathematics, not accuracy
   or speed.

4. Practice should be in terms of correct responses. Errors
   should be eliminated and correct responses reinforced by
   immediate knowledge of the right answer.

5. Practice should be individualized according to the needs or
   ability of the learner, the topic, or the skill involved. The
   learner must be aware of his need to improve.

6. Practice should be relatively brief and at spaced intervals.
   Spaced practice is suggested by retention curves, and brief
   practice is necessary to avoid fatigue.

7. Practice should be given in meaningful exercises so that transfer and application are promoted. If specifics are emphasized
   these should soon be integrated into the whole of which they
   are a part.

8. Practice should be given in a variety of activities. Practice
   lessons may include games, contests, puzzles, timed exercises,
   mental computation, group activities, oral or written exercises.

9. Practice becomes more effective if the learner is informed of
   his progress. The learner should know what competence is
   expected, how he compares with class, school, or national
   norms, and what progress he has made.

10. Practice must never be a punishment. Learning mathematics
    should be a privilege and a pleasant experience. A set of
    exercises should never be assigned as punishment for any
    offense.

Much emphasis is also given in the new programs to learning how to
solve problems. Problem solving is considered an important goal in
mathematics because it is a means whereby:

1. We learn new ideas.
2. We apply our knowledge to a new situation.
3. We transfer ideas and problem solving skill to other fields.

4. We create new knowledge.
5. We practice computational skills.
6. We stimulate intellectual curiosity.

There is really a bit of discovery in the solution of any problem. When a problem arouses your curiosity, it brings into play inventive, creative factors. When you solve the problem you enjoy the experience of success. Experiences such as these will whet the intellectual appetite for more learning of this type. Thus problems are a means of effective discovery teaching.

The modern emphasis on problem solving is on the *method* of solving a problem rather than on the answer. It is the method that can be applied in another situation. It is the analysis that is difficult and needs to be learned. Since every real problem is a novel situation which requires an unknown response, flexibility, originality, and variety of responses are encouraged. As the student searches for a strategy, he is encouraged to make estimations, try hunches, trial and error. He is encouraged to vary the conditions, to visualize the situation, to search for a pattern or relationship.

After the problem is solved, the student is encouraged to extend the problem. He is asked to generalize or interpret the result. He is asked under what conditions the problem would be impossible or when a solution would be meaningless. Finally the student is asked to analyze his method of solution so that he will recognize and use those responses which led to a successful solution.

Mathematics through its ideas and problems is unique in its opportunities for creative, original thinking. Writing original problems, solving problems or establishing theorems with original proofs, discovering and stating relationships in one's own language, drawing an original design are beginning experiences in creative thinking. Communicating mathematical ideas in an original fashion, be it a demonstration, a proof, an exhibit, a poem, or a research project, give further opportunity for originality. The development of a new numeration system, the building of an original model, or the discovery of new ideas or new applications of mathematics illustrate creative work at a higher level. It is the point of view of modern programs that interests, ideas, and questions about new mathematical ideas should be encouraged. Creative students should be provided reading materials, problems, and topics that nourish the exploration of new mathematical ideas.

The new programs are also highly concerned about the development of desirable attitudes, appreciations, and interests. In fact, one of the most frequently used arguments in favor of the new mathematics is the improved attitudes and high interest of students, as well as teachers, using the new programs. The concern for attitudes is also illustrated by the fact that psychologists have been involved in the projects to study attitude formations and instruments to measure attitudes.

Attitudes are recognized as important for several reasons. They largely determine what is learned. We cannot force students to learn something which they reject as not worth the effort. It is the attitudes and interests of students which determine whether or not they will continue the study of mathematics. And it is the attitude and interest in a subject which is highly influential in memory. We remember favorable, pleasant experiences and try to forget unpleasant, frustrating ones.

When studies are made of the reasons for poor attitudes toward mathematics they usually find the following factors:

1. Lack of understanding.
2. Lack of application.
3. Lack of success.
4. Too many boring drill problems assigned daily.
5. Uninspired, impatient, uninteresting teachers.

From our discussions of new programs it is evident that they are all trying to deal with these factors—except possibly the one that involves applications of mathematics.

What kind of teaching is effective in building favorable attitudes? It is the enthusiastic presentation of the elegance, the power, the structure of mathematics. It is teaching that emphasizes discovery, creativity, and curiosity. It is teaching which makes learning a pleasant, successful, and satisfying experience. It is teaching which demonstrates confidence, loyalty, and joy in learning, in teaching, and in working with students. The teacher develops attitudes in his students whether he wants to or not. And the greatest residue of his teaching is likely to be the attitudes which he has nurtured.

SETS

4

One of the hallmarks of the new school mathematics—we can almost say *the* hallmark— is the topic of sets. The language and symbolism of sets are a far cry from the mathematics of yesteryear. But it turns out that this topic is a powerful means for simplifying, clarifying, and unifying mathematics.

One of the surprising things about sets is that the idea does not seem mathematical in nature and, in fact, it is really an idea that we have used frequently without knowing it. A set is simply a collection of things. We may talk of a set of books, of dishes, of furniture, of luggage. Or we may use other words to convey the same idea—a *herd* of cattle, a *pride* of lions, a *troop* of soldiers, a *collection* of stamps, a *group* of statues. In mathematics, we may talk about sets of numbers, points, or measures. From such a simple beginning, we can go on to reach the most profound concepts in mathematics and, in some cases, to arrive at some very startling conclusions that defy common sense.

Sets deal with ideas that pervade all of mathematics. The set idea is one of the basic notions that unifies such apparently diverse mathematical areas as the simple arithmetic of numbers and calculus. One would normally expect that such a fundamental notion would have been discussed by mathematicians in the very early years of the science. But, oddly enough, sets are a very modern mathematical idea. They came into being as a field of mathematics only about a hundred years ago, the contribution of Georg Cantor. Cantor made use of the set idea in proving some very unusual ideas, such as, for example, that there are several sizes of infinities and that a part may be as large as the whole. Soon after Cantor, a British mathematician, George Boole, also became interested in set ideas and developed a little subbranch of mathematics around it. Boole was interested in observing how sets operated, and developed the algebra of sets, also known as *Boolean algebra*.

There are two aspects of sets that concern mathematicians—one, the way sets are useful in the study of all branches of mathematics; and, second, the study of sets as a mathematical phenomenon in their own right. This dual nature of sets has not been clearly understood, and has led to considerable confusion. When we say that youngsters in elementary school should learn about sets, we do not necessarily mean that they should study Boolean algebra. Most often, we mean simply that youngsters should become acquainted with the idea of sets and see how useful it is in all of their work in mathematics. Some of the critics of modern school mathematics attack the whole movement by misinterpreting the purpose of the study of sets. They ask rather scornfully, "Why do fifth-grade youngsters have to study Boolean algebra?" We know of no responsible mathematics educators who suggest that this is a proper activity for fifth graders. Their concern is with the teaching of the other aspect of sets—its use in clarifying and unifying mathematical ideas. Let us see how this works.

We have seen that by a set we mean a collection of things. To a mathematician a set might be a collection of numbers or points on a line.

For convenience, the mathematician uses a pair of braces { } to identify a set. Thus he would indicate the set of even numbers between 0 and 10 like this:

$$\{2, 4, 6, 8\}$$

The set of odd numbers greater than 10 but less than 20 would be written like this:

$$\{11, 13, 15, 17, 19\}$$

To simplify our discussion about a set we usually use a letter as the name of a set. If $S = \{2, 4, 6, 8\}$, we can talk about our set as set S.

SET MEMBERS

The numbers which belong to this set are called the *members* or *elements* of the set. Thus, 2, 4, 6, and 8 are the members of set S. This membership in a set is often designated by the Greek letter epsilon, $\in$. Then the statement "2 is a member of set S" is abbreviated as "$2 \in S$." Likewise, $4 \in S$. But 5 is *not* a member of S, so we write this as "$5 \notin S$."

Frequently we are interested in the number of elements in a set. Set S has four elements. We write this as $n(S) = 4$. If $T = \{11, 13, 15, 17, 19\}$, then $n(T) = 5$.

The two sets we have described above both have a definite number of members. We know that there are only four even numbers between 0 and 10 and only five odd numbers between 10 and 20. Such sets are called *finite sets*. But mathematics is often as concerned with the infinite as it is with the finite, and we need some convenient way of wrestling with the infinite. Suppose we want to talk about the set of counting numbers. We would write it this way:

$$\{1, 2, 3, 4, \ldots\}$$

Here our three dots mean, "and so on, as far as you can go." Many sets of numbers, such as the counting numbers, rational numbers, positive and negative numbers, are all infinite; that is, we could never write the numerals of all the numbers that are members of each of these sets. Yet the idea of sets gives us a means for dealing with them that is very useful.

Now suppose that for every member of one set, we have a corresponding member of another set. Let us say that we have a set of five cats and another set of five milk dishes. Each cat has for his very own one of the milk dishes. We can show this matching relation like this:

$$\{ \text{Cat 1} \quad \text{Cat 2} \quad \text{Cat 3} \quad \text{Cat 4} \quad \text{Cat 5} \}$$
$$\updownarrow \qquad \updownarrow \qquad \updownarrow \qquad \updownarrow \qquad \updownarrow$$
$$\{ \text{Dish 1} \quad \text{Dish 2} \quad \text{Dish 3} \quad \text{Dish 4} \quad \text{Dish 5} \}$$

This says that, for every member of the cat set, there is a corresponding member of the dish set. We say that there is a *one-to-one* correspondence between the two sets. This is not an uncommon situation in everyday life. For every one of the twelve houses on your block there is probably a furnace, so we have a one-to-one correspondence between the set of twelve houses and the set of twelve furnaces. Perhaps there is also a one-to-one correspondence between the twelve houses and twelve first mortgages! When two sets can be matched in this way they are called *equivalent sets*. If they have exactly the same members, we say that the sets are *equal*.

Here again we have a very simple idea that is not especially mathematical in nature. But we will see now that the set idea and the one-to-one correspondence idea give us a true notion of one of the fundamental concepts in mathematics, that of number.

Let us suppose we have a set of four chairs in the dining room:

$$\{C_1 \quad C_2 \quad C_3 \quad C_4\}$$

We also assume we have a set of four people in the family: Father, Mother, Brother, and Sister:

$$\{F \quad M \quad B \quad S\}$$

Now along comes a census taker and, for each member of the family, he makes a tally stroke on his record sheet. This set of strokes would look like this:

$$\{/ \quad / \quad / \quad /\}$$

Each member of one of these sets can be matched with a member of each of the other two sets. Clearly, there is a one-to-one correspondence among all three sets. If, in addition to making the tally marks on his record sheet, the census taker also wrote the numeral 4, you can see that, because of the one-to-one correspondence among the sets, that numeral would also describe the number of members of the other two sets. In fact, it would also describe the number of members of any other set in the world the members of which can also be placed in one-to-one correspondence with any of the sets just mentioned. This, in essence, is what we mean by the number 4—the count of the members of all sets which have a one-to-one correspondence to these tally marks $\{/ \quad / \quad / \quad /\}$ or these family members:

$$\{F \quad M \quad B \quad S\}$$

We can go through the same process and describe in set terms the meaning of all numbers like 1, 2, 3, 5, . . . 599, . . . 6,023, ...

This idea of number is, we hope you agree, not a very complicated one, but it does give concreteness to something that is often otherwise quite foggy, especially to youngsters who are taking their first steps in arithmetic. In fact, this notion of number is being used with some success with very young school children in the new programs in elementary mathematics. With this approach a child can see that there is a concrete quality to sets of, say, five spoons, five dogs, five toy trains, but what joins all of these sets is their quality of "five-ness," which is an abstract matter. No one expects a first grader to be able to verbalize this, but if he has the experience of setting members of sets of five objects into a one-to-one correspondence, it is likely that he will develop a true sense of what the number means—certainly, more of a sense of what it means than we probably did when we were youngsters.

At one pole, sets give us the means to clarify the basic idea of number. At the other end of the scale, sets have enabled us to count the infinite, or at least to put certain limits on it, paradoxical as that may sound.

We said earlier that there is no end to the number of counting numbers. This set is infinite:

$$\{1, 2, 3, 4, \ldots\}$$

We notice that within this set are even numbers, 2 and 4. Is the set of even numbers also infinite? It seems so, for we write this set as:

$$\{2, 4, 6, 8, \ldots\}$$

It is easy to see that these two infinite sets can be put in one-to-one correspondence with each other:

$$\{1, 2, 3, 4, \ldots\}$$
$$\updownarrow \ \updownarrow \ \updownarrow \ \updownarrow$$
$$\{2, 4, 6, 8, \ldots\}$$

But notice that every member of the set of even numbers is contained in the set of counting numbers. We could go on matching members of the two sets, and we would be forced to come to a very odd conclusion—that a part of a set (in this case, the even numbers) has a number to match each member of the entire set (the counting numbers). With this simple analysis, Georg Cantor cast doubt on the previously assumed, often glibly stated, idea that the whole is always greater than any of its parts. When such a seemingly obvious whole can be shown so simply to be *equal* to one of its parts, it is not difficult to understand that other apparently obvious ideas in mathematics may not be so obvious, after all.

Sometimes we are interested in certain members of a set. For example, from set $T = \{1, 2, 3, 4, 5, 6, 7, 8, 9, 10\}$ we may be interested in the even counting numbers less than ten, or set $E = \{2, 4, 6, 8\}$. In this case we say E is a *subset* of T. A subset of a given set is a set that contains all, some, or none of the elements of the given set and contains only elements of the given set. Thus, other subsets of T are $\{3\}$, $\{\ \}$, and $\{1, 2, 3, 4, 5, 6, 7, 8, 9, 10\}$. The set $\{\ \}$ is called the *empty set*. It has no members. It is considered a subset of every set.

SET OPERATIONS

In arithmetic we learned to perform the operations of addition, subtraction, multiplication, and division with numbers. In a similar way we can perform operations on sets. Let us look at these two sets:

{chair, table}   {bed, chest of drawers}

Is there any way that we can combine these two sets of furniture to come up with a set of complete bedroom equipment? We can do this easily by combining or uniting these two sets to form a third set consisting of all the elements in one set or the other, like this:

{chair, table} ∪ {bed, chest of drawers}

$$= \{\text{chair, table, bed, chest of drawers}\}$$

Notice that the symbol ∪ is used to indicate the operation of combining two sets in this fashion. Not surprisingly, this operation is called *union*.

Here are some other examples of the operation of union:

1. N = {houses on north side of our block}
   S = {houses on south side of our block}
   $N \cup S$ = {all houses on our block}
2. A = {numbers less than five}
   B = {numbers greater than or equal to five, but less than ten}
   $A \cup B$ = {numbers less than ten}
3. T = {1, 3, 5, 7, 9}
   E = {2, 4, 6, 8, 10}
   $T \cup E$ = {1, 2, 3, 4, 5, 6, 7, 8, 9, 10}

If you look carefully at these three instances of union, you might suspect that the union operation is quite similar to the operation of addition of numbers. After all, when we add the houses on the north side of the street to those on the south side, we get all the houses on the street, just as we did when we performed the union operation on the two sets of houses.

In point of fact, there is a great similarity between the operation union of sets and addition of numbers. And the new curriculum in arithmetic takes advantage of this similarity to clarify the concept of addition with children. Very often children say, "2 plus 1 is 3," but they really don't know what they are doing. But if we look at sets of objects and perform the operation of union with them, then $\{\triangle, \bigcirc\} \cup \{\square\} = \{\triangle, \bigcirc, \square\}$. From this it follows that:

$$n(\triangle, \bigcirc) + n(\square) = n(\triangle, \bigcirc, \square) \quad \text{or} \quad 2 + 1 = 3$$

Here n stands for "number"; the expression $n(\triangle, \bigcirc)$ is read, "the number of the set, triangle and circle."

We must pause to point out, however, that for the analogy between union and addition to work, we must not have any of the same elements in the sets we are combining. Suppose we had these two sets:

$$A = \{\text{hat, tie, sock}\}$$
$$B = \{\text{shirt, tie, belt}\}$$

Note that the sets have an element in common, tie. When we perform a union operation, we create a new set, the members of which are in *one or another* of the original sets. So, a union of set A and set B would be

$$A \cup B = C = \{\text{hat, tie, sock, shirt, belt}\}$$

The number of elements in set A was 3, and the number in set B was also 3, but the number in set C is 5 not 6 because the tie was in both sets. To illustrate addition in arithmetic, sets that have no elements in common are used, such as

$$A = \{\text{comb, pen}\}$$
$$B = \{\text{watch, belt, button}\}$$
$$A \cup B = C = \{\text{comb, pen, watch, belt, button}\}$$

Then

$$n(A) + n(B) = n(C) = 5$$

Sets like A and B, which have no elements in common, are called *disjoint* sets.

A second operation on sets is the operation of *intersection*. Intersection in sets means pretty much what it means in everyday language. We talk of the intersection of Main Street and Tenth Street. We really mean by this the area that is common to both streets. What, then, is the intersection of these two sets:

$$A = \{1, 2, 3\}$$
$$B = \{3, 4, 5\}$$

If intersection means the elements which are members of both sets, then the intersection of these two sets is clearly 3. We then write the operation symbolically like this:

$$A \cap B = \{3\}$$

The symbol for the intersection operation is $\cap$.

The intersection idea is useful in considering problems like this: Roger, Arthur, and Jack are lawyers. Henry, Dan, and Jack belong to the country club. Who is both a lawyer and a member of the country club? Obviously Jack. We express this symbolically this way:

$$L = \{\text{Roger, Arthur, Jack}\}$$
$$C = \{\text{Henry, Dan, Jack}\}$$
$$L \cap C = \{\text{Jack}\}$$

In the addition of two counting numbers, the sum is always another counting number, as illustrated by $2 + 1 = 3$. In a similar way, the intersection of two sets is always another set.

At this point, we will find it helpful to represent sets by means of pictures. A mathematician named Venn devised this method, and the diagrams which we will use are appropriately called *Venn diagrams*.

For any set, we simply draw a circle and assume that all the elements in the set are contained within the circle. Thus, if set $A = \{1, 2, 3\}$, we show it like this:

If set $B = \{3, 4, 5\}$, we represent it with another circle:

Then we can use Venn diagrams to represent set operations. The union of these two sets, which we know to be $\{1, 2, 3, 4, 5\}$, we show like this:

The intersection of sets A and B, $\{3\}$, is shown like this, with the shaded area indicating the actual intersection:

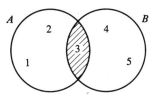

Looking at these diagrams, we can find answers to some basic questions about sets. The first is:

$$\text{Does } A \cup B = B \cup A?$$

This may seem like quite a silly question, but it turns out to be a useful idea. What our question really means is: in performing the union operation, do we get the same result if we start with A and unite it with B as we do when we start with B and unite it with A? Looking at our Venn diagram of union we see that it doesn't seem to make any difference which one we start with. Of course, as mathematicians, we should not be satisfied with this one example as proof, but we can assure you that if you looked at an infinite number of other examples, the result would always be the same. $A \cup B$ is always equal to $B \cup A$. This is one of our basic assumptions in working with sets.

Now let us see whether $A \cap B = B \cap A$. Reference to our Venn diagram and our example indicates that this is true. $A \cap B = \{3\}$ and $B \cap A = \{3\}$. We assume that $A \cap B = B \cap A$ for all cases.

To give this assumption a name, we say that the operations of union and intersection are both *commutative*. Try to remember this word, for we will be using it often later on. In arithmetic certain operations are commutative. We know that in adding two numbers the order of the addition is immaterial. Thus, $1 + 5 = 5 + 1$. And similarly $4 \times 3 = 3 \times 4$. This is a perfectly obvious fact that is not difficult to understand. Youngsters who study under one of the new curriculums now learn the principle of commutativity in their arithmetic and algebra. But many of them often wonder why so much fuss is made about it. This simple principle is one of the foundation stones of mathematical systems. Not all operations are commutative. Thus in arithmetic $4 - 1$ does not equal $1 - 4$, nor is $6 \div 3$ equal to $3 \div 6$. Or, to take an example from everyday life—I am as well dressed if I put my hat on first and then my jacket as I am if I perform these operations in reverse order. But it certainly makes a difference if I put my shoes on first, and then my socks.

We have been talking about sets so far as though they are independent in themselves—sets of a few numbers, for example. But it takes only brief reflection to realize that the numbers that we have chosen are part of a much larger set of numbers. For example, the set

$$\{1, 2, 3, 4\}$$

is part of the set of all counting numbers,

$$\{1, 2, 3, 4, 5, 6, 7, \ldots\}$$

In considering our example of houses on our street, we can see that these houses are actually part of a larger set—the houses in our city, or in our state, or in our country.

In other words, in each case, a set is part of a larger world, or *universe*. In our number example, we can say that our universe is all of the counting numbers and that the four numbers 1, 2, 3, 4 are a *subset* of that universe. If we call the universe U, we can represent this situation with Venn diagrams as follows:

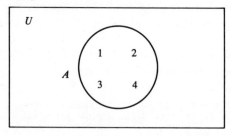

Let us look at this a little more closely. We have a set *A* in a universe *U*. All numbers in the universe are either in set *A* or not in set *A*. Thus the number 4 is in set *A*; the number 5 is not in set *A*. We say that all numbers that are not in set *A* but that are in the universe are part of another set that we may call the *complement* of *A*, or, in symbols, *A'*. Here is a picture of set *A'*. It is represented by the shaded region.

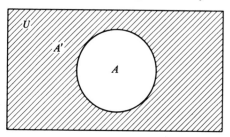

Since every number is in either set *A* or set *A'*, we can see that the union of these two sets is equal to the universe, or:

$$A \cup A' = U$$

Again, you may say that there is nothing particularly startling about this. True, but with these few simple ideas we can develop a number of ideas that are basic not only to sets, but to all of mathematics.

Before we do so, however, we must ask a rather silly question: "How many presidents of the United States were born in Bulgaria?" The answer, obviously, is "none." In set language, we may say that the set of presidents of the United States born in Bulgaria has no members —or, to give it its technical name, is an *empty* set. The symbol for an empty set is $\varnothing$ or, as we have seen, $\{\ \}$. This set corresponds to the number zero. In fact, this is the set that is used to give meaning to the idea of zero.

Here are other examples of empty sets:

1. The set of United States states that begin with the letter "Y."
2. The set of airplanes powered by atomic engines (so far, at least).
3. The set of odd numbers multiplied by 5 which do not end in 5.
4. The intersection of these two sets:

$$A = \{1, 2, 3\}$$
$$B = \{9, 10, 11\}$$

All of these sets would be represented by the symbol $\emptyset$. Thus $A \cap B = \emptyset$.

We now have the tools we need to develop the basic laws referred to above. We have already seen two of the laws:

$$A \cup B = B \cup A \qquad \text{and} \qquad A \cap B = B \cap A$$

For our third law, we need three sets rather than two. Consider these three sets:

$$A = \{1, 2, 3\}$$
$$B = \{4, 5, 6\}$$
$$C = \{7, 8, 9\}$$

In Venn diagrams, they would look like this:

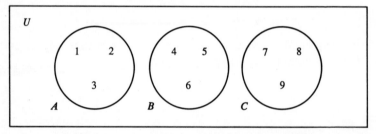

How would we express the union of these three sets? In Venn diagrams the union is represented by the shaded regions.

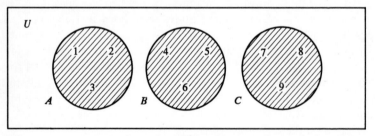

Before we can express the union of the three sets in symbols, we have to realize that union is an operation involving only two sets at a time. We have had experience with this in ordinary arithmetic. When we add three numbers, we add either the sum of the first two to the third or the first to the sum of the second and third:

$$2 + 3 + 4 = (2 + 3) = 5 + 4 = 9$$

or

$$2 + (3 + 4) = 2 + 7 = 9$$

To find the union of sets A, B, and C, we proceed in exactly the same way:

$$A \cup B = \{1, 2, 3, 4, 5, 6\}$$

Then

$$(A \cup B) \cup C = \{1, 2, 3, 4, 5, 6\} \cup \{7, 8, 9\}$$
$$= \{1, 2, 3, 4, 5, 6, 7, 8, 9\}$$

In this example, we have united the two sets, A and B, first, and then united the resulting set with C. Suppose, however, we had united sets B and C and then united that set with A. Would our result have been different? Let us see:

$$B \cup C = \{4, 5, 6, 7, 8, 9\}$$
$$A \cup (B \cup C) = \{1, 2, 3\} \cup \{4, 5, 6, 7, 8, 9\}$$
$$= \{1, 2, 3, 4, 5, 6, 7, 8, 9\}$$

Exactly the same result. We may then state our finding in symbols:

$$A \cup (B \cup C) = (A \cup B) \cup C$$

This simple but important rule we would find holds true in all cases. We call this the *associative property* of the union of sets. Let us see if the operation intersection is also associative.

What is the intersection of these sets:

$$A = \{1, 2, 3\}$$
$$B = \{3, 4, 5\}$$
$$C = \{3, 5, 6, 7\}$$

In Venn diagrams:

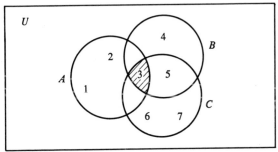

Working with symbols only:

$$A \cap B = \{1, 2, 3\} \cap \{3, 4, 5\}$$
$$= \{3\}$$
$$(A \cap B) \cap C = \{3\} \cap \{3, 5, 6, 7\}$$
$$= \{3\}$$

Let us now start by grouping or associating B and C first:

$$B \cap C = \{3, 4, 5\} \cap \{3, 5, 6, 7\}$$
$$= \{3, 5\}$$
$$A \cap (B \cap C) = \{1, 2, 3\} \cap \{3, 5\}$$
$$= \{3\}$$

We see then that the intersection operation is also associative.

A third basic mathematical law is the *distributive property*. We know from arithmetic that $3 \times (4 + 5) = (3 \times 4) + (3 \times 5)$ since $3 \times (9) = 12 + 15$. We call this the distributive property, or law, of multiplication because, in a sense, the multiplier, 3, is "distributed" over the numbers to be multiplied, $(4 + 5)$.

Not surprisingly, the distributive law has a place in set operations. Suppose we have these three sets:

$$A = \{1, 2, 3, 4\}$$
$$B = \{1, 3, 5, 6\}$$
$$C = \{1, 2, 6, 7\}$$

These sets are shown in Venn diagrams like this:

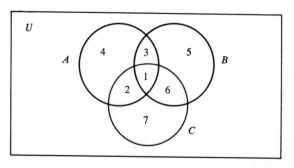

We wish to find out whether the distributive law operates in this case. In other words,

$$\text{Does } A \cap \{B \cup C\} = \{A \cap B\} \cup \{A \cap C\}?$$

In words we read this as "the intersection of set A with the union of sets B and C." From the Venn diagrams, we can see that the union of B and C is $\{1, 2, 3, 5, 6, 7\}$. The intersection of this set with set A is $\{1, 2, 3\}$ so, in symbols:

$$B \cup C = \{1, 3, 5, 6\} \cup \{1, 2, 6, 7\}$$
$$= \{1, 2, 3, 5, 6, 7\}$$
$$A \cap (B \cup C) = \{1, 2, 3, 4\} \cap \{1, 2, 3, 5, 6, 7\}$$
$$= \{1, 2, 3\}$$

If our distributive law holds true, we should also arrive at this result by finding the intersection of A and B and of A and C, and uniting them. In other words, this relationship should hold true:

$$A \cap \{B \cup C\} = \{A \cap B\} \cup \{A \cap C\}$$

We know that $A \cap (B \cup C) = \{1, 2, 3\}$.

$$\{A \cap B\} = \{1, 3\}$$
$$\{A \cap C\} = \{1, 2\}$$

Uniting these two sets, we have:

$$\{A \cap B\} \cup \{A \cap C\} = \{1, 3\} \cup \{1, 2\} = \{1, 2, 3\}$$

This is the same set as $A \cap \{B \cup C\}$ above. Thus the distributive law seems to hold for intersection over union.

In the same way, we could show that the distributive law in the form $A \cup \{B \cap C\} = \{A \cup B\} \cap \{A \cup C\}$ also holds true, but we will omit the details. The ambitious reader may work this out for himself.

To sum up, we have commutative, associative, and distributive laws for the operations union and intersection of sets.

There is another interesting relationship among sets. Consider set A and its complement A'.

By definition the complement of A is everything in the universe U that is not included in A. We have seen that the union of these two sets equals the universe: $A \cup A' = U$. But what is the relationship between A and the universe U? What does $A \cup U$ equal? From the Venn diagram below we can see that the union of A and U is U, or $A \cup U = U$.

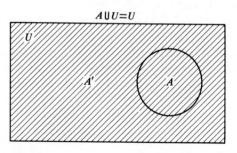

Then what does $A \cap U$ equal? Obviously this equals A.

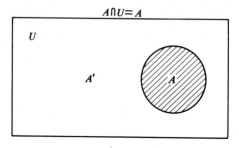

How are sets A, U, A', and $\varnothing$ related? If you stop to think you will realize that $A \cap A' = \varnothing$, $A \cup \varnothing = A$, and $A \cap \varnothing = \varnothing$. Look again at the last two set equations, $A \cup \varnothing = A$ and $A \cap \varnothing = \varnothing$. Remembering that $\varnothing$ means the empty set, does this remind us of a similar situation in arithmetic? In the operation of addition, is there a number that can be added to another, say 4, that will give us the same number, 4, as an answer? Or, to put the question another way: $4 + ? = 4$.

One need not be talented mathematically to see that our question mark can be replaced by 0, for, $4 + 0 = 4$. Because the 0, when added to 4, produces identically the same answer as if we had not performed the operation at all, we call 0 the *identity element* in addition. In a similar way, $\varnothing$ is the identity element for union, since $A \cup \varnothing = A$.

In arithmetic we also have an identity element for multiplication:

$$4 \times ? = 4$$

Here the number 1 gives us our answer:

$$4 \times 1 = 4$$

So 1 is our identity element for multiplication. What is the identity element for intersection? Since $A \cap U = A$, it would seem to be U.

We have touched upon these set operations and relations for several reasons. First, from a simple idea of grouping objects into sets, we can, with a little ingenuity, build up a whole catalog of relations among sets. More important than this, we have developed certain laws or properties and put them into operation. These are laws that a student of mathematics from a modern point of view comes upon again and again in his studies. They are principles that underlie many systems of mathematics. We have in this discussion drawn analogies between the way these laws operate with sets and with the numbers of arithmetic. We shall soon see that our system of arithmetic is indeed built upon these laws, as are other systems of mathematics, such as matrices and vectors, which we shall not go into in this book.

Since these laws will be referred to many times from here on, we repeat them here:

	Arithmetic	*Sets*
1. Commutative law, or law of order	$4 + 5 = 5 + 4$	$A \cup B = B \cup A$
	$4 \times 5 = 5 \times 4$	$A \cap B = B \cap A$
2. Associative law, or law of grouping	$4 + (5 + 6)$ $= (4 + 5) + 6$	$A \cup \{B \cup C\} = \{A \cup B\} \cup C$
	$4 \times (5 \times 6) = (4 \times 5) \times 6$	$A \cap \{B \cap C\} = \{A \cap B\} \cap C$
3. Distributive law	$4(5 + 6) = (4 \times 5) + (4 \times 6)$	$A \cap \{B \cup C\} = \{A \cap B\} \cup \{A \cap C\}$
		$A \cup \{B \cap C\} = \{A \cup B\} \cap \{A \cup C\}$
4. Identity element	$4 + 0 = 4$	$A \cup \varnothing = A$
	$4 \times 1 = 4$	$A \cap U = A$

SET APPLICATIONS

Perhaps some of you will be tempted to ask whether this is the only answer to why all the fuss is made over sets. There are many other applications of the set idea, and we will come across them time and again in this book, but for the impatient, we can cite a few uses here, without going into great detail.

1. The algebra of sets, which we have touched upon only briefly, has great practical application in the field of electronic computers. The electric circuits of the computers can be represented by the set operations of union and intersection. The

union ($A \cup B$) operation represents switches in parallel circuits and the intersection ($A \cap B$) operation represents switches in series.

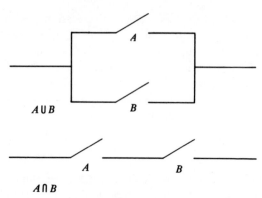

$A \cup B$

$A \cap B$

Just how do the operations of union and intersection apply to these switches? Remember that the union operation on sets A and B produces a third set whose members are in *either A or B*. In the parallel circuit shown at the top, when *either* switch A or switch B is closed, the electric current may flow on through the wire. On the other hand, in the intersection operation on set A and set B, a third set is produced whose members are in *both A and B*. In the circuit with switches in series, at the bottom of the drawing, *both* switch A *and* switch B must be closed for current to flow on through the wire.

2. In logic, which is being increasingly studied in mathematics, the set notion gives us a useful tool for showing the relationship between statements. For example, suppose we wish to test the logic of these three related statements:

A = all women are beautiful creatures.

B = all wives are women.

C = therefore, all wives are beautiful creatures.

Let A, B, C be thought of as sets. Then the relationship is shown as follows:

A = a universal set, the set of all beautiful creatures.

B = the set of all women.

C = the set of all wives.

In Venn diagrams:

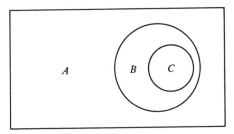

In set notation:

$A \cap B = B$ means that all women (B) are a subset of A (all
    women are beautiful creatures).

$B \cap C = C$ means that all wives (C) are included in set B and
    hence are women.

$A \cap C = C$ means that all wives (C) are included in set A and
    hence are beautiful creatures.   This is what we
    wish to prove.

3. We will come across numerous examples of the set idea in
   algebra. We may mention one here; namely, the universe concept.   Suppose we are asked to find a value for x in this
   equation:

$$x + 5 = 2$$

(If you have forgotten what this means, this mathematical
sentence can be read as "What number (x) when added to 5
will result in a sum of 2?") If our universal set consists of the
whole numbers of arithmetic,

$$U = \{0, 1, 2, 3, 4 \ldots\}$$

we must conclude that the replacement for x consists of an
empty set, for no number in set U when added to 5 will yield 2.
But if our universal set includes positive and negative numbers,

$$U = \{\ldots {}^{-}5, {}^{-}4, {}^{-}3, {}^{-}2, {}^{-}1, 0, 1, 2, 3, 4 \ldots\}$$

then we can find a replacement for x that will make $x + 5 = 2$
a true statement. The number from the set that qualifies is ${}^{-}3$,
for

$$^{-}3 + 5 = 2.$$

4. Set ideas in geometry are not hard to come by. The notion of intersection has a ready application that a geometry student meets in his first week in the course. The intersection of line *l* and line *m* in this drawing is point *C*, or *l* ∩ *m* = *C*.

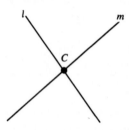

In general the intersection of two lines consists of a point; the intersection set of one plane and another plane is a line. What kind of set describes the intersection of parallel lines (in Euclidean geometry, that is)?

We hope that in reading this chapter you have found that learning the new mathematics can be a pleasant experience. The ideas are not difficult if you read thoughtfully and are not frightened by new symbols. You will probably need to read about mathematics differently from the way you would read a story. Read slowly, use a pencil to try examples of your own, and then practice on the exercises at the ends of chapters, beginning here. The answers are given in the appendix so that you may have a ready way of checking your progress.

EXERCISES

1. Are the following sets infinite, finite, or the empty set?
   a. The atoms in the earth and its atmosphere.
   b. The number of even thousands, for example, 1000, 2000, and so forth.
   c. The set of foreign-born presidents.
   d. The set of numbers divisible by 13.
   e. The intersection of the set of boys and the set of girls.
2. Which of the following statements are true?
   a. A subset of {*a, b, c*} is {*a*}.
   b. There is a one-to-one correspondence between the counting numbers and the grains of sand on our earth.
   c. If *A* is the set of vowels, then *U* is the set of consonants.

    d. If E is the set of even counting numbers, then E' is the set
       of odd counting numbers.

    e. If $n(A) = n(B)$ then A and B have the same elements.

3. What are the answers to these operations?

    a. $A \cap A' =$

    b. $A \cup U =$

    c. $A \cup \varnothing =$

    d. $A \cap \varnothing =$

    e. $A \cap U =$

4. If $A = \{a, b, c, d\}$, $B = \{a, c, e, g\}$, and $C = \{a, d, e, f\}$,
   what are the members of these sets?

    a. $A \cup B =$

    b. $A \cap B =$

    c. $B \cap C =$

    d. $A \cap \{B \cup C\}$

    e. $A \cup \{B \cap C\}$

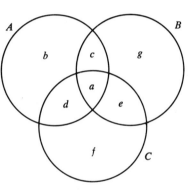

5. Find the number of elements in each subset as illustrated by this Venn diagram.

    a. $n(A)$

    b. $n(A \cup B)$

    c. $n(A \cup B \cup C)$

    d. $n(A \cap C)$

    e. $n(A \cap B \cap C)$

6. Draw Venn diagrams to illustrate the set operations in Exercise 4 above.

NUMBERS, NUMBER SYSTEMS, AND
MATHEMATICAL STRUCTURES

5

Are numbers a new idea in school mathematics? Obviously not. We all began the study of arithmetic by learning to count and compute. What can possibly be new about numbers?

What is new about numbers is not that new numbers or new operations have been discovered. Rather the new programs in mathematics introduce new language and new ideas about the nature of numbers and how we operate with them. The emphasis is on a few basic properties of numbers and operations which extend to all fields of mathematics.

Before we begin to consider number systems, we need to clarify our thinking about what a number means and what a numeral means. The new school mathematics programs make a special point about establishing the difference between "number" and "numeral." The reason for this emphasis is to clarify our language and, consequently, our thinking.

Briefly, a number refers to an idea—the idea of three-ness, four-ness, or the square-root-of-two-ness. A numeral, on the other hand, is a way of representing the idea of a number. A numeral is a name for a number. Here are some numerals for the number three:

$$3, \text{ III}, 2 + 1, 7 - 4, 6 \div 2, \sqrt{9}$$

We need to have the true meanings of number and numeral clearly in mind; otherwise, we may not be able to comprehend ideas such as these:

1. 5 as a number is larger than 3.
2. 5 as a numeral may or may not be larger than the numeral 3.
   Thus, in this instance, (5, **3**), 5 is smaller than **3**.

The University of Illinois Committee on School Mathematics places a great deal of emphasis on the distinction between number and numeral, and early in its first course students are asked to evaluate statements like these:

> If we take 5 away from 53, the result is 3.
>
> Half of 8 is 3 (8).
>
> If we add 9 to 7, the result is 79.

As the course proceeds, students are expected to continue to make the distinction between number and numeral. Those who use "number" when they mean "numeral" are regarded as mathematical pariahs. Other programs, however, are satisfied to establish the distinction at the outset and then bow to the inevitable interchangeable use in popular parlance. We shall attempt here to be consistent in differentiating between number and numeral.

We have seen that number as an idea can be defined in terms of sets. A counting number describes the common property of sets which have a one-to-one correspondence. The number three, for example, describes the one-to-one correspondence that exists among sets like these:

$$\begin{array}{ccc} \{\text{apple,} & \text{pear,} & \text{orange}\} \\ \updownarrow & \updownarrow & \updownarrow \\ \{\text{boy,} & \text{baby,} & \text{man}\,\} \\ \updownarrow & \updownarrow & \updownarrow \\ \{1, & 2, & 3\,\} \end{array}$$

These sets have a common property which we call "three-ness." Each set is said to have three elements. Any other set which can be matched with these sets by a one-to-one correspondence is said to have three elements. Sometimes we say the number of elements in a set determines the *cardinal number* of the set. The cardinality of the sets above is 3. When these sets are matched with the set of counting numbers arranged in order from left to right, the last counting number on the right gives the cardinality of the matching set.

$$\begin{array}{cccccc} A = & \{\text{bat} & \text{ball} & \text{mitt} & \text{glove} & \text{mask}\} \\ & \updownarrow & \updownarrow & \updownarrow & \updownarrow & \updownarrow \\ B = & \{1 & 2 & 3 & 4 & 5\,\} \\ \end{array}$$
$$n(A) = n(B) = 5$$

Actually, primary school teachers used this idea in building concepts of numbers long before they had heard of modern mathematics. They have used collections (sets) such as sticks, cards, or marbles to illustrate the idea of number. However, the counting process often got mixed up with the number concept. Later the numbers were not distinguished from their names or numerals.

Present-day programs recommend the continued use of sets of objects in developing number concepts. With a one-to-one matching, it is easy to find how one group compares with another, which number is larger than another and how much larger. This matching then brings out another important aspect of numbers, namely, order. How do we know that one number is smaller than another? How can we arrange the numbers in order from the smallest to the largest?

New programs are also getting at this order of numbers by the use of a *number line*. A line is marked off into equally spaced points, much like a ruler. Then the points are named by numbers in their natural or consecutive order.

This line pictures the relationship of one number to another and at the same time suggests, by the use of the arrow, that there is no largest number.

COUNTING NUMBERS

The counting numbers are, naturally enough, the numbers we use when we count objects. They are members of the set $\{1, 2, 3, 4, \ldots\}$. One of the first things that we may notice about our counting numbers is that every member has a next or succeeding counting number. This fact is so obvious that it must come as a surprise to know that this was first set down as a property of the system only about 80 years ago, by an Italian mathematician named Giuseppe Peano (1858–1932). Perhaps other people had noticed the same thing about the counting numbers but thought this was such a trivial observation that it wasn't worth putting down on paper. But Peano, being a modern mathematician, was interested in understanding the structure of the number system, and an understanding of the structure includes an understanding of the axioms or assumptions on which the structure rests.

Peano also noted a few other rather obvious but axiomatic ideas about this counting number system. One of them was that there is one number in the system that is the successor of no counting number; namely, the number 1. It was necessary for Peano to make this statement because without such an axiom this system might have looked like this,

where 1 is the successor of 8.

One would think that these two axioms would be sufficient for such a simple system as the counting numbers but Peano wished to guard against two other eventualities that might develop. He had to prevent a situation like this from holding true:

$$1 \rightarrow 2 \rightarrow 3 \searrow \atop 6 \quad\; 4 \atop \searrow 5 \swarrow$$

Here both 2 and 6 have the same successor, 3. To rule this out, Peano assumed that if two counting numbers have the same successor, then these two counting numbers must be identical.

One further difficulty remained to be taken care of—the existence of the counting numbers in the form $\{A, B, C, 1, 2, 3, 4, \ldots\}$. This might happen with this arrangement:

$$1 \rightarrow 2 \rightarrow 3 \rightarrow 4 \ldots$$
$$A$$
$$C \qquad B$$

To rule this out Peano adopted the fourth assumption: If the set of counting numbers contains the counting number 1 as a member and also contains the successor of each of its members, then it contains *all counting* numbers.

In developing these four simple axioms or assumptions, Peano did for arithmetic what Euclid, two thousand years earlier, had done for geometry. Experimental programs do not suggest that the Peano postulates be studied by young children when they are introduced to the counting numbers. But we have introduced them here in part as a demonstration of the building of a mathematical system on basic assumptions which is so characteristic of the mathematics of our day.

Once the basis of the counting number system has been established, it is possible for mathematicians to define the operations of arithmetic in terms of the basic axioms. We shall be content to mention that this has been done and proceed to discuss the operations themselves and other characteristics of the counting number system. In doing so we shall bring up once again the axioms or principles we developed earlier in connection with set theory, plus a few new ones.

We are dealing with the set of counting numbers:

$$C = \{1, 2, 3, 4, 5, 6, 7 \ldots\}$$

Let us add any two numbers in this set, say 3 and 4:

$$3 + 4 = 7$$

No matter how we find the sum of 3 and 4, it is always 7 and no other number.

Let us try again, with 23 and 255:

$$23 + 255 = 278$$

Both sums, 7 and 278, are counting numbers. In fact, if we add *any* two numbers in this set, we get as a sum another specific counting number. In general, if *a*, *b*, and *c* are members of the set of counting numbers, $a + b = c$. When a situation like this holds true, we say the set is *closed*. The set of counting numbers is closed with respect to addition. We can't get outside the set of counting numbers by adding two counting numbers.

Is the set of counting numbers closed with respect to multiplication?

$$2 \times 3 = 6 \qquad 4 \times 12 = 48$$

Try as long as we may, we cannot find a product of two counting numbers that is not a member of the set. So, $a \times b = c$, where *a*, *b*, and *c* are counting numbers, and the set is closed with respect to multiplication.

Is the set closed for subtraction?

$$10 - 2 = 8 \qquad 26 - 21 = 5$$

We know that 8 and 5 are members of the set. But what about $2 - 10$ and $21 - 26$? No answers can be found which are in the set. Thus the counting numbers are *not* closed with respect to subtraction.

And division?

$$10 \div 5 = 2 \qquad 65 \div 5 = 13$$

But $10 \div 3$ and $20 \div 7$? Clearly the set is *not* closed for division.

Is the set of even counting numbers closed with respect to addition? Yes, because the sum of two even counting numbers is always another even number.

Is the set of odd counting numbers closed with respect to addition? No, because the sum of two odd counting numbers is always an even number.

In our discussion of sets, we considered certain properties of union and intersection such as the commutative property, associative property, and distributive property. For set operations we found that:

1. $A \cup B = B \cup A$
   $A \cap B = B \cap A$

   The operations of union and intersection are commutative.

2. $A \cup (B \cup C) = (A \cup B) \cup C$
   $A \cap (B \cap C) = (A \cap B) \cap C$

   The operations of union and intersection are associative.

3. $A \cap (B \cup C) = (A \cap B) \cup (A \cap C)$
   $A \cup (B \cap C) = (A \cup B) \cap (B \cup C)$

   The operation of intersection is distributive over union, *and* the operation of union is distributive over intersection.

Now we can quickly examine the operations of addition and multiplication in the set of counting numbers to see whether these properties hold true.

Since $3 + 5 = 5 + 3$, we assume that for any two counting numbers (a and b), $a + b = b + a$. Two counting numbers may be added without regard to the order in which we add them. This is the *commutative property* for addition in the set of counting numbers.

Likewise $3 \times 5 = 5 \times 3$, so we assume that for any two counting numbers (a and b), $a \times b = b \times a$. Two counting numbers may be multiplied without regard to the order in which we multiply them.

This is the *commutative property* for multiplication in the set of counting numbers.

Thus we assume that in the set of counting numbers addition and multiplication are commutative.

Aside from being an important property of our number system, commutativity enables us to check our computations, in this way:

Addition:

Adding down	*Adding up*
8	8
+7 ↓	+7 ↑
15 = 8 + 7	15 = 7 + 8

Multiplication:

78		43
×43		×78
234	or	344
312		301
3354		3354

When we perform additions and multiplications, we always work with two numbers at a time. Thus we say addition and multiplication are *binary* operations. When more than two numbers are involved, we use grouping symbols to tell us the order in which to perform the binary operations.

$(3 + 4) + 2 = 7 + 2 = 9$ $\qquad\qquad (3 \times 5) \times 8 = 15 \times 8 = 120$

and

$3 + (4 + 2) = 3 + 6 = 9$ $\qquad\qquad 3 \times (5 \times 8) = 3 \times 40 = 120$

Since $3 + (4 + 2) = (3 + 4) + 2$, we assume that for any counting numbers $(a, b,$ and $c)$, $a + (b + c) = (a + b) + c$. In other words, for addition of counting numbers the way in which we group into pairs of numbers does not affect the sum. This is the *associative property* of addition in the set of counting numbers.

Similarly, since $3 \times (5 \times 8) = (3 \times 5) \times 8$, we assume that for any counting numbers $(a, b,$ and $c)$, $a \times (b \times c) = (a \times b) \times c$. For the multiplication of counting numbers, the way in which we group into pairs of numbers does not affect the product. This is the *associative property* of multiplication in the set of counting numbers.

Hence we assume that in the set of counting numbers, addition and multiplication are associative.

The associative property can be used to explain and check some computations like these:

1. Addition of a column

Add down		*Add up*	
4		4	
5	↓	5	↑
6		6	
15 = (4 + 5) + 6		15 = (6 + 5) + 4	

2. Addition with two-digit numerals

$$34 = 30 + 4$$
$$+57 = 50 + 7$$
$$80 + 11 = 91$$

3. Subtraction with two-digit numerals

$$53 = 40 + 13$$
$$-36 = 30 + \ 6$$
$$10 + \ 7 = 17$$

Compare the results for computations that involve both multiplication and addition.

$$3 \times (4 + 5) = (3 \times 4) + (3 \times 5) = 12 + 15 = 27$$
$$3 \times (9) = 27$$

We express this property as follows:

$$a \times (b + c) = (a \times b) + (a \times c),$$

where *a*, *b*, and *c* are counting numbers.

This is the *distributive property* of multiplication over addition in the set of counting numbers. Note that we do *not* assume that addition is distributive over multiplication. Since $3 + (4 \times 5)$ is not equal to $(3 + 4) \times (3 + 5)$, this counterexample is sufficient evidence to eliminate the assumption that $a + (b + c)$ and $(a + b) \times (a + c)$ are equal.

The distributive property is basic to an explanation of our multiplication process.

1. $\begin{aligned} 7 \times 43 &= 7 \times (40 + 3) \\ &= (7 \times 40) + (7 \times 3) \\ &= 280 + 21 \\ &= 301 \end{aligned}$

2. $\begin{aligned} 35 \times 63 &= 35 (60 + 3) \\ &= (35 \times 60) + (35 \times 3) \\ &= (30 + 5) \times 60 + (30 + 5) \times 3 \\ &= (30 \times 60) + (5 \times 60) + (30 \times 3) + (5 \times 3) \\ &= 1800 + 300 + 90 + 15 \\ &= 2205 \end{aligned}$

Finally, we must observe one other property of the counting number system. Is there a number that serves as an identity element with respect to addition or multiplication? What number when added to or multiplied by another natural number will yield that number as sum or product?

$$5 + ? = 5$$
$$4 + ? = 4$$

We suspect that the number 0 will work here, but we must restrain ourselves because the number 0 is not in the set of counting numbers.

What about multiplication?

$$5 \times ? = 5$$
$$4 \times ? = 4$$

The number 1 will fill our need, and 1 *is* in the set of counting numbers. So the set of counting numbers has 1 as the identity element for multiplication. There is no identity element for addition in the set of counting numbers.

Let us summarize the characteristics of the set of counting numbers in the table below, where a, b, c, and d are counting numbers.

Property	Addition	Multiplication
1. Closure	$2 + 3 = 5$	$3 \times 8 = 24$
	$a + b = c$	$a \times b = d$
2. Commutative property	$3 + 5 = 5 + 3$	$7 \times 8 = 8 \times 7$
	$a + b = b + a$	$a \times b = b \times a$
3. Associative property	$(7 + 8) + 3 = 7 + (8 + 3)$	$(2 \times 7) \times 5 = 2 \times (7 \times 5)$
	$(a + b) + c = a + (b + c)$	$(a \times b) \times c = a \times (b \times c)$
4. Distributive property		$5 \times (8 + 4) = (5 \times 8) + (5 \times 4)$
		$a \times (b + c) = (a \times b) + (a \times c)$
5. Identity element		$3 \times 1 = 3$
		$a \times 1 = a$

WHOLE NUMBERS

Historically, one of man's aims in mathematics has been to build number systems with greater and greater versatility. Since the set of counting numbers did not have an identity element for addition, man had to invent one. To us in the latter half of the twentieth century this would not seem to be a difficult task. But the fact is that it was not until after the beginning of the Christian Era that this new element was invented. This element was the number zero. With zero, we have an identity element for addition:

$$4 + 0 = 4$$
$$a + 0 = a$$

When zero is included in the set of counting numbers, we have a new set, which we call the set of *whole numbers.*

$$W = \{0, 1, 2, 3, 4, \ldots\}$$

Since this set includes the counting numbers as a subset, it is reasonable to assume that all the properties of addition and multiplication in the set of counting numbers also apply to this set. Of course, we have one new property; namely, an identity element for addition.

The set of whole numbers has some members which have some unusual characteristics. Take zero for example. When zero is added to a number, the sum is the number: $a + 0 = a$. When zero is subtracted from a number, the result is the same: $a - 0 = a$. When a number is multiplied by zero, the product is always zero: $a \times 0 = 0$.

When zero is divided by a number, the quotient is always zero: $0 \div a = 0$. Thus, zero is the only number which can be divided by every other number without a remainder. However, we must be careful not to divide by zero. A basic commandment in mathematics is "Thou shalt not divide by zero." Division by zero is said to be undefined. The reason for this is as follows: Suppose we could divide by zero. Then $a \div 0 = b$. If the quotient of $a \div 0$ is b, then $a = b \times 0$. But the product of $b \times 0$ is 0. There is no quotient b which when multiplied by zero will equal a. Likewise $0 \div 0$ is declared meaningless. If $0 \div 0 = a$ then a could be any number because the product of any number and zero is zero.

Another interesting number is the number 1. It has many useful properties. We have already mentioned that the product of a number multiplied by 1 is the number: $a \times 1 = a$. Likewise, the quotient of a number divided by 1 is the number: $a \div 1 = a$. The number 1 is the only number which is an exact divisor of every number. The quotient of a number divided by itself is also 1: $a/a = 1$. And 1 is the only number of which no other counting number is an exact divisor.

These properties of 1 have been found useful in many ways. Here is how we use them to find new numerals for fractional numbers.

$$\frac{1}{2} = \frac{1}{2} \cdot 1 \qquad \text{What property of 1 is this?}$$

$$\frac{1}{2} \cdot 1 = \frac{1}{2} \cdot \frac{3}{3} \qquad \text{What property of 1 is this?}$$

Since $\frac{1}{2} \cdot \frac{3}{3} = \frac{3}{6}$, then $\frac{1}{2} = \frac{3}{6}$

Of course, 1 is in the spotlight too because it is the building block of our number system. Beginning with 1, all counting numbers are formed by adding 1; for example, $2 = 1 + 1$, $3 = 2 + 1$, $4 = 3 + 1$, and so on.

Now that we have learned the characteristics of some numbers, let us take another look at operations. How do we define the operations of addition, subtraction, multiplication, and division?

In our discussion of sets we learned that addition is related to the union of two disjoint sets. Addition is the operation that combines the cardinal numbers of two disjoint sets to give the cardinal number of the union of these disjoint sets. If $A = \{a, b, c\}$ and $B = \{x, y\}$, then $n(A) + n(B) = n(A \cup B)$. Since $n(A \cup B) = n(a, b, c, x, y) = 5$, then $3 + 2 = 5$.

Addition, of course, is also related to counting. To get the sum of $3 + 4$, you count to 3 and continue to count 4 more successors until you get to 7. This counting is also related to taking trips on the number line. Beginning at 0 a trip of 3 units and then 4 more units will take you to the 7 point on the number line.

An extremely modern program in arithmetic may also describe addition in a rather different way, involving what is called a *mapping* process. Look, for example, at these Venn diagrams:

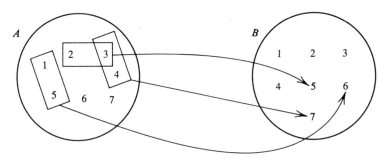

Here, in set A pairs of numbers are grouped and mapped to numbers in set B which are the sums of the numbers in each pair. We can also describe this description of addition as a example of a *two-to-one* correspondence.

Traditionally, subtraction was thought of as a "take-away" process. The subtraction $7 - 3$ was translated into words as "seven take away three." Youngsters studying modern arithmetic are encouraged to think of this problem as, "What number added to three will give seven?" In other words, subtraction is thought of in terms of addition, rather than as a completely separate or different operation. Modern thinking proceeds like this: If $3 + 4 = 7$, then $7 - 4 = 3$ or $7 - 3 = 4$. In other words, $a = c - b$ if $a + b = c$. In this sense, we say that subtraction is the *inverse* of addition. If 8 has been added to 5 to give a sum x: $(5 + 8) = x$ then we "undo" this addition by the subtraction of 8: $(5 + 8) - 8 = x - 8$, or $5 = x - 8$.   An understanding of this relationship, then, reduces the number of different number facts that a pupil must remember. If a pupil knows that $8 + 5 = 13$, and that subtraction "undoes" addition, he need not memorize $13 - 8 = 5$ and $13 - 5 = 8$ as separate facts.

Is there a commutative property for subtraction?

$$\text{Does } 7 - 3 = 3 - 7?$$

Clearly, no.

Is there an associative property for subtraction?

$$\text{Does } (7 - 5) - 3 = 7 - (5 - 3)?$$

Again, no.

Is the set of whole numbers closed under subtraction? Does $7 - 3$ equal a whole number? Yes. Does $5 - 8$ equal a member of our set of whole numbers? No. This one counterexample is enough for us to reject closure for the whole numbers under subtraction.

In order to get a set of numbers which is closed with respect to subtraction, we must invent some new numbers. We shall say that $1 - 2 = {}^{-}1$ and $1 - 3 = {}^{-}2$, and so on. Of course, we could also say that $3 - 4 = {}^{-}1$ or $7 - 8 = {}^{-}1$, and many others. We will call this new number set $\{{}^{-}1, {}^{-}2, {}^{-}3, \ldots\}$ the set of *negative numbers*. Notice that we write the negative numbers as ${}^{-}1, {}^{-}2, {}^{-}3$, rather than $-1, -2, -3$. We do this to distinguish between the numeral ${}^{-}1$, which we identify as "negative 1," and the operation -1, which means subtract 1.

We cannot relate the meaning of these numbers to the count of elements of a set; instead, we illustrate the order of the negative numbers with a number line, like this:

Notice that the numbers to the right of zero are now considered positive numbers, and are identified by the positive sign $+$. For each counting number, there is a corresponding positive number. And for each positive number there is a corresponding negative number. When we add zero to this set (zero is neither positive nor negative), we have the set of *integers*.

$$I = \{\ldots\, {}^{-}3, {}^{-}2, {}^{-}1, 0, {}^{+}1, {}^{+}2, {}^{+}3 \ldots\}$$

Since the positive integers have the same order on the number line as counting numbers, it is customary to omit the + symbol for positive integers. Thus, $^+3$ is represented by 3. The context of the situation usually tells us whether the "3" represents the integer $^+3$ or the counting number 3.

We can investigate the set of integers with respect to the operations of addition, subtraction, multiplication, and division by operating with specific integers. When we do this we find that the commutative, associative, and distributive properties hold. The set of integers is closed with respect to addition, subtraction, and multiplication, but not division ($\frac{12}{7}$ has as a quotient no number in the set of integers). There is an additive inverse for each element of the set: for example, $^+3 + {}^-3 = 0$, but there is still no inverse for multiplication.

What does multiplication mean? Usually we have considered multiplication as a shortcut for addition. Thus 3×4 means the sum of 3 fours or $3 \times 4 = 4 + 4 + 4$. Another approach to multiplication is to relate it to arrays. An array is an arrangement of objects in columns and rows. Then 3×4 can be considered an array of 3 rows with 4 in each row or 4 rows with 3 in each row.

We count the total objects, to get the product 12. These arrays also illustrate the commutative property of multiplication.

Another way to explain multiplication is to combine the elements of sets. Suppose $A = \{a, b, c\}$ and $B = \{w, x, y, z\}$. Form the set of all the possible pairs by using one element from each set for each pair. We get

$$C = \{aw, ax, ay, az, bw, bx, by, bz, cw, cx, cy, cz\}$$

Then we say set C is the *cross product* of A and B, or $A \times B = C$, and $n(A) \times n(B) = n(C)$. Hence the product of two numbers is the number of elements in the cross product of two sets.

Multiplication can also be related to the union of sets. Then 3×4 means the union of 3 disjoint sets of 4 members each. As with addition, multiplication can also be considered a mapping process. Since

$(3 \times 4) \rightarrow 12$, $(2 \times 6) \rightarrow 12$, $(1 \times 12) \rightarrow 12$, it is a many-to-one mapping.

Modern mathematics defines division as the inverse of multiplication. If $3 \times 4 = 12$, then $12 \div 3 = 4$ and $12 \div 4 = 3$. In general terms, if $a \times b = c$, then $b = c \div a$ or $a = c \div b$ (provided a and b are different from zero). This inverse relationship means that division "undoes" multiplication. If 6 has been multiplied by 5, (6×5) to give a product p, $(6 \times 5 = p)$, then we "undo" this multiplication by division by 5: $(6 \times 5) \div 5 = p \div 5$ or $6 = p \div 5$.

Division as the inverse of multiplication is described as repeated subtractions of the same number. Division can also be considered as a way of forming subsets—subsets with the same number of elements. This relationship then reduces the number of facts a pupil must remember. If he knows that $5 \times 8 = 40$, he also knows that $40 \div 5 = 8$ and $40 \div 8 = 5$.

The distributive property of division over addition is illustrated by these patterns:

$$\frac{6 + 1 = 7}{5\,)\overline{30 + 5}}$$

$$\begin{aligned}
168 \div 12 &= (120 + 48) \div 12 \\
&= (120 \div 12) + (48 \div 12) \\
&= 10 + 4 \\
&= 14
\end{aligned}$$

Is there a commutative property for division? Does $12 \div 4 = 4 \div 12$? Obviously, no.

Is there an associative property for division? Does $(12 \div 6) \div 2 = 12 \div (6 \div 2)$? No.

Much has been made recently of a new method of division now used in many modern programs. When you went to school you were probably taught to handle this division problem

$$23\,)\overline{828}$$

like this:

1. Find the largest number of times 23 will go into 82 (or 2 into 8). After some surreptitious figuring at the side of

your paper, you come up with 3 and proceed to do the following:

$$\begin{array}{r} 3 \\ 23\overline{)828} \\ -69 \\ \hline 138 \end{array}$$

2. You now repeat the process, dividing 23 into 138. Again, after much trial and error, you find the proper quotient and write:

$$\begin{array}{r} 36 \\ 23\overline{)828} \\ -69 \\ \hline 138 \\ -138 \\ \hline 0 \end{array}$$

The new method is designed to eliminate the need to perform separate preliminary divisions. Here is how the new method would look with the same problem:

$$\begin{array}{r|r} 23\overline{)828} & \\ -460 & 20 \\ \hline 368 & \\ -230 & 10 \\ \hline 138 & \\ -\ 92 & 4 \\ \hline 46 & \\ -\ 46 & 2 \\ \hline 0 & 36 \end{array}$$

Instead of finding a partial quotient that fits the partial dividend, the student actually guesses how many 23's are contained in the whole dividend, 828. In the example above his first estimate is 20. He then subtracts the part of the dividend he has already used up (460) and starts again with the remainder, 368. He repeats the process, and when he has exhausted his remainders, he adds up his partial quotients. Clearly, this method, while perhaps somewhat longer than the method we learned in school, is more direct and less conducive to mechanical error. Of course, with this method many variations of the solution are possible:

23)828			23)828	
−115	5		−230	10
713			598	
−115	5		−230	10
598			368	
−115	5		−230	10
483			138	
−230	10		−115	5
253			23	
−230	10		− 23	1
23			0	36
− 23	1			
0	36			

What is the mathematical basis for this method of division? It is simply an application of the fact that division is distributive over addition. Our three variations of the division

$$\frac{828}{23}$$

can be summarized like this:

1. $\dfrac{828}{23} = \dfrac{460 + 230 + 92 + 46}{23}$

   $= \dfrac{460}{23} + \dfrac{230}{23} + \dfrac{92}{23} + \dfrac{46}{23}$

   $= 20 + 10 + 4 + 2 = 36$

2. $\dfrac{828}{23} = \dfrac{115 + 115 + 115 + 230 + 230 + 23}{23}$

   $= \dfrac{115}{23} + \dfrac{115}{23} + \dfrac{115}{23} + \dfrac{230}{23} + \dfrac{230}{23} + \dfrac{23}{23} = 36$

3. $\dfrac{828}{23} = \dfrac{230 + 230 + 230 + 115 + 23}{23}$

   $= \dfrac{230}{23} + \dfrac{230}{23} + \dfrac{230}{23} + \dfrac{115}{23} + \dfrac{23}{23} = 36$

RATIONAL NUMBERS AND IRRATIONAL NUMBERS

With our set of integers—negative and positive whole numbers and zero—division is closed only for certain pairs of integers, such as $^+15 \div {}^+3 = {}^+5$ and $^-21 \div {}^+7 = {}^-3$. However, $^+3 \div {}^+4$ does not give a quotient which is an integer. The quotient is $^+\frac{3}{4}$. This quotient is a number which is called a *rational number*. In everyday arithmetic we called it a fraction. The new mathematics considers the fraction a numeral. Hence the rational number $^+\frac{3}{4}$ may be expressed by many fractions such as $^+\frac{6}{8}$, $^+\frac{15}{20}$, and so on. A rational number then is a quotient expressed as a/b, where a and b are integers and b is not 0. Integers can be expressed as quotients, too. For example,

$$^+2 = \frac{^+8}{^+4}, \qquad ^-3 = \frac{^-15}{^+5}, \qquad \text{and} \qquad 0 = \frac{0}{^-2}$$

Hence the set of rational numbers includes all the integers.

We now have a set of numbers, the rational numbers, which is closed with respect to all the fundamental operations. Each member of this set also has an inverse for multiplication, as illustrated by these examples:

$$^+2 \times {}^+\tfrac{1}{2} = {}^+1 \qquad ^-\tfrac{3}{4} \times {}^-\tfrac{4}{3} = {}^+1$$

Finally, we wish to consider, though briefly, one other set of numbers, called the *irrational numbers*. They are given this name, not because there is something illogical or insane about them, but because they cannot be expressed as the quotient of two integers; that is, as rational numbers. Included in the set of irrational numbers are such numbers as $\sqrt{2}$, $\sqrt{3}$, and π (the quotient of the circumference of a circle and its diameter, called "pi"). Taken together, the set of rational numbers and the set of irrational numbers make up the set of *real numbers*.

MATHEMATICAL STRUCTURES

We have seen that our various number systems have certain properties—commutativity, associativity, distributivity, and so forth, with respect to certain operations. Modern mathematics, in its effort to generalize systems as much as possible, has given particular names to systems which have certain characteristics. The various number systems we have discussed have characteristics of what are known as *groups*, *rings*, and *fields*. While these terms have common meanings in everyday speech, in modern mathematics they have very particular meanings, as we shall soon see. The properties of various mathematical systems, such as number systems, taken together, comprise the *structure* of that system. Modern mathematics is very much interested in the structures of mathematical systems because in examining these structures we uncover similarities among systems that one would never suspect existed. For example, the set of rational numbers has a certain structure. Who would suspect that the set of rational numbers and a system of certain operations that we can perform with an ordinary file card that is marked like the one below have much in common?

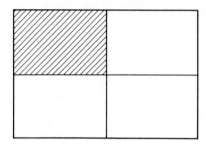

But before we examine this odd similarity, we must re-examine the set of rational numbers.

Let us consider the set of rational numbers and one operation, multiplication. What are the properties of the rational numbers as related to multiplication?

Are the rational numbers *closed* with respect to multiplication? Yes. Every product of two rational numbers is another rational number. For example,

$$\frac{2}{3} \times \frac{1}{5} = \frac{2}{15} \quad \text{and} \quad \frac{7}{4} \times \frac{3}{3} = \frac{21}{12}$$

Does the *associative property* apply to the multiplication of rational numbers? Yes. For example,

$$\frac{2}{3} \times \left(\frac{4}{5} \times \frac{7}{7}\right) = \left(\frac{2}{3} \times \frac{4}{5}\right) \times \frac{7}{7}$$

Does the set of rational numbers have an *identity element* for multiplication? Is there a number, *n*, such that $a/b \times n = a/b$? Yes, it is 1. For example,

$$\frac{3}{4} \times 1 = \frac{3}{4} \quad \text{and} \quad \frac{a}{b} \times 1 = \frac{a}{b}$$

Does the set of rational numbers have an *inverse* with respect to multiplication for every rational number? Is there a number, *n*, such that $a/b \times n = 1$? Yes. Since

$$\frac{a}{b} \times \frac{b}{a} = \frac{ab}{ba} = \frac{ab}{ab} = 1$$

the multiplicative inverse of a/b is b/a. We say b/a is the *reciprocal* of a/b. Thus for $\frac{3}{4}$ the reciprocal is $\frac{4}{3}$ and $\frac{3}{4} \times \frac{4}{3} = 1$. However, there is one exception. There is no reciprocal for 0.

We now have the six requirements for a mathematical *group*, as follows:

Requirements	*Example*
1. A set of elements.	1. The set of rational numbers.
2. An operation.	2. Multiplication.
3. The set of elements is closed with respect to the operation.	3. The product of two rational numbers is another rational number.
4. The operation is associative.	4. The grouping of the rational numbers in multiplication does not change the product.
5. There is an identity element for the operation.	5. The identity element for multiplication is 1, or $a/b \times 1 = a/b$.
6. There is an inverse of the operation for each element of the set.	6. The multiplicative inverse for each rational number is its reciprocal (except for 0); the multiplicative inverse of a/b is b/a, where $a \neq 0$ and $b \neq 0$.

Note that while the rational numbers are commutative, this characteristic is not a requirement for qualification as a group. Some groups are commutative; others are not.

In a similar way, other sets of numbers, such as the counting numbers, the integers, and the irrational numbers can be examined with respect to one operation—addition or multiplication—to see if they are examples of mathematical groups.

But you may be wondering what this has to do with operations with this card:

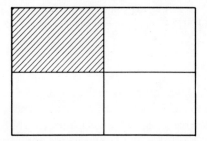

We are going to turn the card in various ways and then see whether there is any kind of pattern or structure to our turns. Assume that the card is marked on front and back with the shaded portion in exactly the same position on each side like a flag. Assume also that we are going to rotate the card (that is, turn it so that its other side shows) around one of its two axes. One axis is vertical:

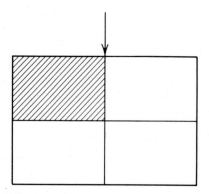

The other axis is horizontal:

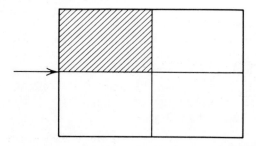

Another way we will rotate the card is around an imaginary pin located at the intersection of the horizontal and vertical axes:

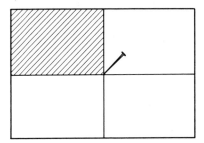

Suppose we call the starting position *position a*.

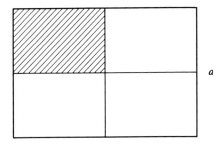

a

A rotation of 180° around the vertical axis turns the card over and gives us *position b:*

b

Starting again with position *a*, we now rotate 180° around the horizontal axis and arrive at *position c:*

c

Starting once more with *position a,*

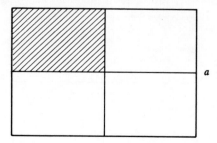

we turn the card on the imaginary pin 180° to *position d:*

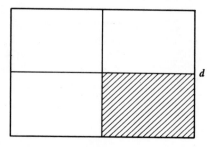

We have used three ways of rotating:

1. *Rotation from position a to position b*—rotation of 180° on the *vertical* axis.
2. *Rotation from position a to position c*—rotation of 180° on the *horizontal* axis.
3. *Rotation from position a to position d*—rotation of 180° in the same plane.

We can also consider one further operation:

4. *Rotation from position a to position a*—no rotation. (Question for the mathematically alert: How is this rotation related to the identity element in the operation of multiplication with rational numbers?)

Now we are ready to perform these rotations. We will keep notes on our operations, but, in characteristic mathematical fashion, we will use some symbols for the sake of brevity. For the operation of rotation we will use the symbol *. Then

$$a * b \rightarrow b$$

means that we start with position a, rotate 180° on the vertical axis, and find that our card comes to rest in position b. Note that the rotation designated by * depends on the letter that follows it.
Then

$$b * c \rightarrow d$$

means that we start with position b, rotate 180° on the horizontal axis, and come to rest in position d.
Then

$$d * a \rightarrow d$$

means that, starting with position d, rotation a will keep us in position d.
In order to follow our discussion, it would be useful for the reader actually to make up a file card for the operations called for in our system. The two sides of his card should look like this:

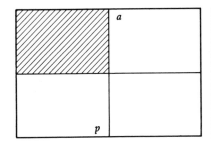 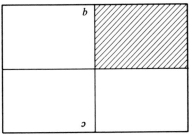

Now see whether you can verify these "rotation equations":

$$b * b \rightarrow a$$
$$b * d \rightarrow c$$
$$c * c \rightarrow a$$
$$d * d \rightarrow a$$
$$b * d \rightarrow c$$

We can now put all the possible rotations into a neat little table for the operation, just as we do for an operation like multiplication with counting numbers.

*	a	b	c	d
a	a	b	c	d
b	b	a	d	c
c	c	d	a	b
d	d	c	b	a

With this table we can readily find the results of our rotations. For example, to get the result of $c * d$ we find c in the column at the left, locate d in the top row, then note where c and d intersect. We see b in the box, so

$$c * d \rightarrow b$$

We are, seemingly, a very long way from the idea of a group, but we will now proceed to head rapidly back in that direction by asking, and answering, a series of questions:

1. Is it true that every time we perform a rotation operation, we get as an answer one of the positions, a, b, c, or d? Clearly, this is true, so we can say our set of elements $\{a, b, c, d\}$ is closed with respect to the rotation operation.
2. Suppose we have to perform these operations:

    a. $(a * b) * c$

    b. $a * (b * c)$

    Would our result be the same in each case? In other words, is the rotation operation associative? Let us see.

    a. $(a * b) * c = b * c \rightarrow d$

    b. $a * (b * c) = a * d \rightarrow d$

    We can see that the rotation operations are, in fact, associative.
3. If we have a certain position, which rotation must we perform

to get back to that position? In other words, what is the solution set for the equations

$$c * x \rightarrow c$$
$$b * x \rightarrow b$$
$$d * x \rightarrow d$$
$$a * x \rightarrow a$$

Is there any doubt that the solution set is *a*? In other words, *a* is an identity element for the rotation operation.

4. Now, how do we undo an operation? In other words, starting with a position such as *b*, how can we get back to position *a*? Or

$$b * x \rightarrow a$$

Or

$$c * x \rightarrow a$$
$$d * x \rightarrow a$$
$$a * x \rightarrow a$$

In each instance the solution set is the rotation operation that bears the same letter as the position involved. For example, in $b * x \rightarrow a$, $x = b$. Looking back at our table of operations on page 80, we can see that for every row there is an element *a*. It is clear, then, that for the rotation operation we have an inverse for each element of our set.

The answers to the questions we have just answered add up to the fact that our system is a group with respect to the rotation operation. Let us set up a table that compares this group with the rational numbers as a group:

Requirements	Position System	Rational Numbers
1. A set of elements.	Positions *a, b, c, d*.	All numbers of the form *a/b*.
2. An operation.	Rotation.	Multiplication.
3. The set of elements is closed with respect to the operation.	The result of the operation in any position is one of the positions: for example, $a * b \rightarrow b$.	The product of two rational numbers is another rational number.

Requirements	Position System	Rational Numbers
4. The operation is associative.	The grouping of the positions in the operation does not change the result; for example, $(a * b) * c = a * (b * c)$.	The grouping of the rational numbers in multiplication does not change the product: $(a \times b) \times c = a \times (b \times c)$.
5. There is an identity element for the operation.	The identity element is rotation a; for example, $b * a \rightarrow b$.	The identity element for multiplication is 1, or $a/b \times 1 = a/b$.
6. There is an inverse of the operation for each element of the set.	The operational inverse for each position is its rotational counterpart; for example, $b * b \rightarrow a$.	The multiplicative inverse for each rational number is its reciprocal (except for 0), or $a \times 1/a = 1$.

When a set of elements involves two operations, such as addition *and* multiplication, we may have mathematical structures called rings or fields.

For a set to qualify as a ring, it must be commutative under one operation. Further, with reference to the second operation, the set must be closed, associative, and distributive over the first operation. We can see that our set of rational numbers qualifies also as a ring, with respect to the operations of addition and multiplication. Why does our system of card operations *not* qualify as a ring?

For a set of elements to qualify as a field, it must have all of the characteristics of a ring, plus an identity element and an inverse element for the second operation and be commutative for the second operation. Again, the set of rational numbers qualifies as a field with respect to addition and multiplication. In fact, so does the set of real numbers.

We have seen that, with respect to a group, the properties that characterize a group are not necessarily limited to numbers. We have seen, too, that sets and the set operations of union and intersection obey some of the same laws as some number systems. You might wish to see for yourself whether sets qualify as groups, rings, or fields with respect to the operations of union and intersection.

Now that we have taken the time and space to develop the characteristics of these number systems, you may still be dubious as to their usefulness and purpose. Actually this treatment of the number systems serves several functions. The basic properties of the fundamental operations apply to many topics farther up the line. The study of fractions and decimals, the solution of equations, the factoring of algebraic expressions, and the rules for operating on positive and negative numbers are examples of ideas that can be made reasonable using these basic properties. Basic definitions and assumptions are always used to establish every topic of mathematics as a logical structure. It is assumed that knowing the structure of a topic will help the student remember it, apply it in a new situation, and use it to invent or discover a new topic.

Let us see how some of the ideas covered in this chapter relate to some of the questions we raised on pages 4 and 5 in Chapter 1.

1. When we divide $\frac{1}{2} \div \frac{1}{4}$, why do we invert the divisor, $\frac{1}{4}$, and multiply?

   a. If $\frac{1}{2} \div \frac{1}{4} = q$ then $\frac{1}{2} = q \times \frac{1}{4}$
   b. If $\frac{1}{2} = q \times \frac{1}{4}$ then $\frac{1}{2} \times \frac{4}{1} = q \times \frac{1}{4} \times \frac{4}{1}$
   c. If $\frac{1}{2} \times \frac{4}{1} = q \times \frac{1}{4} \times \frac{4}{1}$ then $\frac{1}{2} \times \frac{4}{1} = q$

2. $37 - 9 = (30 + 7) - 9$
   $= 20 + (10 + 7) - 9$
   $= 20 + (17 - 9)$
   $= 20 + 8$
   $= 28$

3. $43 \times 67 = (40 + 3) \times (60 + 7)$
   $= (40 + 3) \times (60) + (40 + 3) \times (7)$
   $= (40 \times 60) + (3 \times 60) + (40 \times 7) + (3 \times 7)$
   $= 2400 + 180 + 280 + 21$
   $= 2881$

4. $\dfrac{12}{0.2} = \dfrac{12}{0.2} \times 1 = \dfrac{12}{0.2} \times \dfrac{10}{10} = \dfrac{120}{2} = 60$

5. How many $\frac{1}{8}$'s in $\frac{1}{4}$, or $\frac{1}{4} \div \frac{1}{8} = ?$

$$\tfrac{1}{4} = \tfrac{1}{4} \times 1 = \tfrac{1}{4} \times \tfrac{2}{2} = \tfrac{2}{8} = 2 \cdot \tfrac{1}{8}$$

Hence there are two $\frac{1}{8}$'s in $\frac{1}{4}$.

6. $\frac{1}{6} + \frac{1}{12} = (\frac{1}{6} \times 1) + \frac{1}{12} = (\frac{1}{6} \times \frac{2}{2}) + \frac{1}{12} = \frac{2}{12} + \frac{3}{12} = \frac{5}{12}$

7. $\$1.00 - \$0.65 = x$, or $1.00 = x + .65$ by the definition of subtraction.

8. $^{+}5 + {}^{-}5 = 0$ and $^{-}3 \times 0 = 0$

   Hence $^{+}3 \times (^{+}5 + {}^{-}5) = 0$. By the distributive property we have $^{-}3 \times {}^{+}5 + (^{-}3 \times {}^{-}5) = 0$. Since $^{-}3 \times {}^{+}5 = {}^{-}15$, then $^{-}15 + (^{-}3 \times {}^{-}5) = 0$. Since $^{-}15 + {}^{+}15 = 0$, then $^{-}3 \times {}^{-}5 = {}^{+}15$.

9. $\dfrac{7.68}{4.2} = \dfrac{7.68}{4.2} \times 1 = \dfrac{7.68}{4.2} \times \dfrac{10}{10} = \dfrac{76.8}{42}$

10. $\dfrac{3}{4} = \dfrac{3}{4} \times 1 = \dfrac{3}{4} \times \dfrac{25}{25} = \dfrac{75}{100}$

EXERCISES

1. Which of the following represent zero?
   a. 2×0 d. $5 - 5$
   b. $\frac{1}{0}$ e. $\frac{4}{4}$
   c. $\frac{0}{2}$

2. Which of the following computations cannot be performed?
   a. $0 \div 5$ d. $\frac{0}{6}$
   b. 0×0 e. $\frac{8}{0}$
   c. $0 + 9$

3. Which of the following are numerals for 1?
   a. $\frac{2}{3} \div \frac{2}{3}$ d. $1 - 0$
   b. $\frac{1}{0}$ e. $1 \times 1 \times 1$
   c. $\frac{3}{4} \times \frac{4}{3}$

4. Consider the set of even integers

$$E = \{ \ldots {}^{-}6, {}^{-}4, {}^{-}2, 0, {}^{+}2, {}^{+}4, {}^{+}6, {}^{+}8, \ldots \}.$$

   a. Is set E closed with respect to addition?
   b. Is set E closed with respect to multiplication?
   c. What is the identity element for addition?

   d. What is the identity element for multiplication?
   e. What is the additive inverse for zero?
5. Give an example illustrating that each statement is true.
   a. Negative five ($^-5$) is a rational number.
   b. Zero is a rational number.
   c. The sum of two rational numbers may be equal to one.
   d. The product of two rational numbers may be equal to one.
   e. The quotient of two rational numbers may be equal to one.
6. Write three fractions to represent each of these rational numbers.
   a. $\frac{2}{3}$ d. 1.6
   b. $^-1$ e. $-\frac{5}{8}$
   c. 5
7. Which of the following statements are true?
   a. The sum of two integers is always another integer.
   b. The additive inverse for $^-7$ is 0.
   c. The multiplicative inverse for $^-3$ is $-\frac{1}{3}$.
   d. If $x + 5 = 0$, then $x = {}^-5$.
   e. If $a \div b = x$, then $x = b \div a$.
8. Select the property which is illustrated by these equalities.
   a. $(8 + 9) + 7 = 8 + (9 + 7)$ I. Commutative property
   b. $(6 + 3) + 5 = (3 + 6) + 5$ II. Associative property
   c. $(4 \times 7) + 1 = 1 + (4 \times 7)$ III. Distributive property
   d. $8 \times (5 + 6) = (8 \times 5) + (8 \times 6)$
   e. $(8 \times 7) \times 9 = 8 \times (7 \times 9)$
9. Find the value of x by using the properties or definitions of this
   chapter. Indicate the property or definition used.
   a. $x + 7 = 7 + 9$
   b. $(6 + x) + 8 = 8 + (6 + 5)$
   c. $5(x + 3) = 20 + 15$
   d. $8x = 96$
   e. $x - 17 = 42$

NUMERATION SYSTEMS

6

One of the most baffling topics to parents whose children are involved in the new school mathematics is the work with numerals in various bases. It is frightening to a grown man, a product of American schools, sane in mind and sound in body, a pillar of his community, to learn suddenly that $2 + 2 = 10$. If $2 + 2$ does not equal 4, are our schools teaching nonsense in mathematics? For the benefit of all distraught parents, we would like to offer the reassurance that two plus two does indeed equal four, and when the teacher of modern mathematics says $2 + 2 = 10$, he is simply reaffirming the truth of what we all learned at school about two plus two. But he is, in a sense, using a different language to say it.

Recall our discussion in the last chapter of the difference between number and numeral. As numbers, two plus two will always equal four. But when we write the numerals $2 + 2 = 10$, we are using 10 as a new numeral for four. The numbers are the same; it is only the way we represent them—their numerals—that has changed.

These new numerals for numbers—*numeration systems*, we call them —seem to fascinate youngsters because in a sense they give a completely new look at number ideas. After they have had their first lesson in new number bases, youngsters love to confront their parents with their new knowledge. To adults the topic seems difficult because we have never considered the possibility of numerals different from our own. It has never seemed necessary or desirable to use a system other than our decimal, or base-ten, system. Why should we not consider the possibility that there are numerals better than our Hindu-Arabic system, which is only about 1500 years old?

The use of numerals to represent numbers is a great invention. History tells us that man first kept count of objects with pebbles, or tally marks, or his fingers. He used a one-to-one correspondence between objects such as his sheep and marks on a stick. When man began to record his ideas in writing, he invented symbols to represent numbers. Here are some of the numerals that have been used in the past to record a count of twenty-three objects:

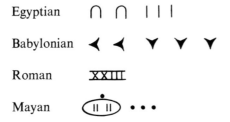

Egyptian

Babylonian

Roman

Mayan

A numeration system consists of a certain number of symbols and some orderly process by which the symbols are used to represent numbers. The most widely used numeration systems in man's history have been able to represent many different numbers with a few symbols. These numerals have made it possible to perform certain operations with numbers. Our own numeration system is called a *base-ten system*, because the basis of its operation is the grouping of items or elements into tens and groups of tens.

Why do we use ten as a basis for our grouping? Ten as a base probably derives from the fact that we have ten fingers on our two hands. Many hundreds of years ago, before the advent of numerals, it was probably customary for people to tick off the number of items in a set on their fingers, using one-to-one correspondence between finger and object. When they ran out of fingers, they knew they had a complete set of ten objects.

You may wonder why they did not continue counting on after ten, to twenty, using their toes. At least one people, the Mayans of ancient Mexico, did just that. To them a group was complete only when it contained twenty objects. Their system, then, was a base-twenty system. The ancient Babylonians chose to use a base-sixty system. Some primitive tribes have used a base-five system, probably because they considered only the fingers of one hand. In other words, there is nothing sacrosanct about our use of ten as the basis for our system. People have used other bases, and, in fact, as we shall soon see, there are distinct disadvantages to the base-ten system.

Before we talk about other systems, we need to examine our own system in greater detail. We all know that one of the neat aspects of our system is that we can represent any number, no matter how small or how large, by using only ten basic symbols, called *digits*: 0, 1, 2, 3,

4, 5, 6, 7, 8, 9. The count represented by each digit depends on its position in a numeral. Examine these six numerals:

164

146

461

416

641

614

Each of these numerals represents a different number, yet, we have used only three digits for all six numbers. What determines the value of each digit is its position in the numeral. In the numeral 164, the 4 means 4 units; in 146, the 4 means 4 tens; in 461, the 4 means 4 hundreds. In other words, the numeral 461 is really a compound affair that consists of these parts: $400 + 60 + 1 = 461$. We commonly assign a name to each of the positions or places in a number such as 461:

hundreds	tens	units
4	6	1

A system like this, where the value of a digit depends on its place in a numeral, is called a *place-value system*. Not every system of numeration is a place-value system. Recall the Roman system, for example, where twenty-one is shown as XXI. Each symbol represents a specific value, and that value is dependent only partly on its position in the numeral. This holds true even in a number such as XIX. Here both X's are tens and the I is one, but the position of the I before the second X means that it is to be subtracted from the second X, rather than added, as in XXI.

Our place-value system would not be possible unless we had a way of indicating when we had a count of zero for a particular group. Leaving spaces for a place without a value can lead to all sorts of confusion. Perhaps 9   3 would be clear enough for a number with an empty set of groups of tens, but how many groups with empty sets are indicated in this number?

9   3

With the invention of the digit zero (0) (which, by the way, first appeared in manuscripts in the ninth century A.D.), we have a way of showing just which groups have an empty set count of zero. Now we can readily see the difference between 903 and 9003.

We are now almost ready to take a look at systems with bases other than ten, but we must first remind ourselves of one or two other matters. First, the size of the groups counted by each digit of a numeral is related. Each group counted by a digit in a numeral is increased in multiples of ten. The count of groups by each digit is related to each other digit by a multiple of ten; and ten is the base of our system.

In order for a symbol to have different values, we use it to count groups. These groups are of different sizes. The size of the groups in a numeration system is what is referred to as the *number base*. In our system we group in tens so we say it is a base-ten system. It is also called a decimal system, the word "decimal" coming from the Latin word for ten.

Let us represent the number twenty-three with marks:

$$\boxed{XXXXXXXXXX}$$
$$\boxed{XXXXXXXXXX}\ XXX$$

We have 2 groups of ten and 3 left over. We write this as 23, which really means 2 tens and 3, or $2 \times (10) + 3$.

For larger numbers we collect groups of tens. Here is how we arrange the marks that represent the number one hundred thirty-five in this system.

$\boxed{XXXXXXXXXX}$		
$\boxed{XXXXXXXXXX}$		
$\boxed{XXXXXXXXXX}$		
$\boxed{XXXXXXXXXX}$		
$\boxed{XXXXXXXXXX}$		
$\boxed{XXXXXXXXXX}$		
$\boxed{XXXXXXXXXX}$		
$\boxed{XXXXXXXXXX}$	$\boxed{XXXXXXXXXX}$	
$\boxed{XXXXXXXXXX}$	$\boxed{XXXXXXXXXX}$	
$\boxed{XXXXXXXXXX}$	$\boxed{XXXXXXXXXX}$	XXXXX
100	30	5
10 tens	3 tens	5 ones
10×10	3×10	5×1

Notice that we have thirteen groups of ten, but we have gathered ten of these groups into a larger "bundle" to make a hundred. Thus $135 = 100 + 30 + 15 = 1 \times (10 \times 10) + 3 \times (10) + 5$.

Second, we must clearly understand that we have no *single* digit that stands for the base of our system. We write ten as 10. The numeral "10" says we have no units but only 1 group of ten. Likewise, when we consider other bases, the numeral "10" will always represent the base of these systems.

We have already mentioned that other groupings besides ten have been used in our history—five, twenty, and sixty, for example. In fact, *any* counting number may be used as a base. (We should exempt 1, of course, because grouping by ones is like tallying and gets us absolutely nowhere, numerationally speaking.) Our only requirements for a system with any number as base are the following:

1. A number symbol to represent each of the unit values.
2. A value relationship of each symbol of the numeral to the base number.

THE BASE-FIVE SYSTEM

Let us start our exploration of other bases with five as a base. Five then becomes the base of our grouping system.

In base ten we had ten digits, 0, 1, 2, 3, 4, 5, 6, 7, 8, 9. Base five should then reasonably have five digits:

$$0, 1, 2, 3, 4$$

	Numeral representing the number
One object	*of objects in our set*
X	1
Two objects	
XX	2
Three objects	
XXX	3
Four objects	
XXXX	4

So far, there is no difference between base five and base ten. But we shall now have to perform our first grouping operation:

$$XXXXX$$

We have one group of five. How do we show this as a numeral? How many ungrouped units are there? None. We therefore need a zero in units place. How many groups of five do we have? One. Therefore, we need a 1 in the "fives" place. So our numeral should say 1 five and no more. In base five we write this as 10 base five. (To keep our bases straight we shall from now on indicate the base as a subscript. A count of five objects in base five is therefore 10_{five}.) Be sure to note that 10_{five} means 1 group of five and no ones. Then 11_{five} means 1 group of five and 1 more. Which of the following shows 23_{five}?

$$(XXXXX)$$

$$(XXXXX) \quad XXX$$

$$XX \quad XXX$$

$$\binom{XXXXX}{XXXXX} \quad XXX$$

From here on, it is easy to build up our base-five system. All we must keep in mind is that in a numeral of more than one digit, each digit counts a group that is *five* times greater than the group counted by the next digit to the right. Thus 342_{five} is:

five × five	fives	ones
3	4	2

What numeral in the base-ten system would represent 342_{five}? We should be able to make use of the values of each base-five place to find our answer.

$$342_{five} \quad = 300_{five} + 40_{five} + 2$$

Base five				*Base ten*
300_{five}	$= 3 \times$ five $\times$ five	$=$	75
40_{five}	$= 4 \times$ five	$=$	20
2	$= 2$	$=$	2
			97

Notice that our base-ten numeral is "smaller" (has fewer digits) than its base-five equivalent. Is this reasonable? It is reasonable in the sense that 97 has fewer groups, but each group has more elements than the base-five groups indicated by the numeral 342_{five}.

Here is a table that shows how grouping by fives gives us base-five numerals.

Base-ten numeral	Base-five grouping			Base-five numeral	Base-five name
3	*XXX*			3	three
5	*XXXXX*			10_{five}	one five
8	*XXXXX*	*XXX*		13_{five}	one five and three
17	*XXXXX*			32_{five}	three fives and two
	XXXXX	*XX*			
	XXXXX				
24	*XXXXX*	*XXXX*		44_{five}	four fives and four
	XXXXX				
	XXXXX				
	XXXXX				
25	*XXXXX*			100_{five}	one five times five
	XXXXX				
	XXXXX				
	XXXXX				
	XXXXX				
41	*XXXXX*	*XXXXX*	*X*	131_{five}	one five times five, three fives and one
	XXXXX	*XXXXX*			
	XXXXX	*XXXXX*			
	XXXXX				
	XXXXX				

One way to make the base-five system more meaningful is to relate it to pennies, nickels, and quarters. Suppose that we have 4 of each of these coins. If we make change with the least number of coins we will have an example of base-five numerals.

Amount of money in cents	Quarters	Nickels	Pennies	Base-five numeral
7		1	2	12_{five}
13		2	3	23_{five}
24		4	4	44_{five}
36	1	2	1	121_{five}
69	2	3	4	234_{five}
98	3	4	3	343_{five}

Now that we know what base-five numerals mean, we should be able to perform some computations with them. However, the purpose of these computations is merely to focus attention on the computational process and the meaning of numerals. There is no point in taking the time to become proficient in computing in base five.

In principle, fundamental operations in any base are not difficult. They follow base-ten operations in all respects. Here is an example of base-five addition and its rationale:

$$
\begin{array}{rl}
14_{five} = & 1 \text{ five and 4 ones} \\
23_{five} = & 2 \text{ fives and 3 ones} \\
\hline
42_{five} = & 3 \text{ fives and 7 ones} = 4 \text{ fives and 2 ones}
\end{array}
$$

You may wish to do the following additions on your own. (A good way to check is to convert each numeral into the base-ten system and add.)

43_{five} 23_{five} 242_{five}
21_{five} 14_{five} 113_{five}

If extended work in one number base is to be done, the class often constructs an addition table. This provides a ready reference source. A base-five addition table is shown at the right.

+	1	2	3	4	10
1	2	3	4	10	11
2	3	4	10	11	12
3	4	10	11	12	13
4	10	11	12	13	14
10	11	12	13	14	20

Subtraction, we have already seen, is now thought of as the inverse of addition. To solve the problem

$$11_{\text{five}}$$
$$\underline{-2_{\text{five}}}$$

we ask, "What number added to 2 will give 11_{five}?" Using the addition table already constructed, we find the $2_{\text{five}} + 4_{\text{five}} = 11$, so we know that $11_{\text{five}} - 2_{\text{five}} = 4_{\text{five}}$. Of course, one good way to investigate addition and subtraction is to use a number line with base-five numerals.

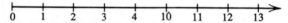

Multiplication in base five would be a needless chore to youngsters if they had to memorize all of the basic multiplication facts. Fortunately, as in base ten, multiplication in base five can be thought of as repeated addition. With this as a tool, multiplication tables can be constructed which then serve as reference points. Here is part of the multiplication table in base five; the reader may exercise his other-base muscles by completing it:

×	1	2	3	4	10
1	1	2	3		
2	2	4	11		
3	3	11	14	22	
4	4	13			
10					

To extend the table to larger numbers we use the distributive property.

$$3 \times 34_{\text{five}} = 3 \times (30_{\text{five}} + 4_{\text{five}})$$
$$= (3 \times 30_{\text{five}}) + (3 + 4)$$
$$= 140_{\text{five}} + 22_{\text{five}}$$
$$= 212_{\text{five}}$$

If you wish to multiply by the traditional vertical arrangement, be careful of place value and "carrying."

$$\begin{array}{cc} 34_{\text{five}} & 23_{\text{five}} \\ 3 & 2 \\ \hline 212_{\text{five}} & 101_{\text{five}} \end{array}$$

The multiplication table is quite indispensable in division problems. Division, we recall, is the inverse of multiplication, so a problem like $11_{\text{five}} \div 3$ can be thought of as, "What number multiplied by 3 gives 11_{five}?" Our table shows us that $3 \times 2 = 11_{\text{five}}$, so $11_{\text{five}} \div 3 = 2$.

THE BASE-TWELVE SYSTEM

As we indicated earlier, the precise bases which youngsters study vary from program to program. Either base five or base seven is the system usually used to introduce the other-base concept. Base twelve and base two are also studied, for each has certain particular properties that reveal special aspects of numeration systems.

Twelve, with its multiples, is a base that is used in several common measuring systems—we group some objects by dozens and gross (12 doz.), we have 12 in. in a foot, 3×12 in. is a yard, 60 min. in an hour, 360° in a circle, and the English have twelve pence in a shilling. Just why these measuring schemes should be in use, we are not sure, but a reasonable explanation for the comparative popularity of 12 as a base is that 12 can be evenly divided by more counting numbers than can 10. The only factors of 10 (aside from itself and 1) are 5 and 2; 12 has twice as many factors: 2, 3, 4, 6. This characteristic has led a certain group of enthusiasts (The Duodecimal Society of America) to campaign for the replacement of our base-ten (decimal) system by a base-twelve (duodecimal) system.

Aside from the number of factors of 12, the duodecimal system is interesting to operate in for it requires the invention of two additional symbols. Base twelve requires 12 symbols; we have only 10 available from the decimal system, giving us numerals through 9. For 10, the letter X is usually used, and for 11, E is supplied. Thus, in the duodecimal system we run into such numerals as $1E_{\text{twelve}}$ and $EX4_{\text{twelve}}$. [Where $1E_{\text{twelve}} = 1 \times (12) + 11$, and $EX4_{\text{twelve}} = 11 \times (12 \times 12) + (10 \times 12) + 4$.]

Twelve is the only system commonly studied which has a base larger than ten. This means that a numeral in the duodecimal system will look as though it is "smaller" than one of the same value in the decimal system. For example, $2148_{ten} = 12E0_{twelve}$; $439_{ten} = 307_{twelve}$. The reason why this should be so is an interesting one for youngsters to consider, and should add further to their understanding of the many possibilities man has at his disposal to represent numbers.

THE BASE-TWO SYSTEM

The numeration system with the smallest possible number of digits is the base-two system; it consists of only two digits, 0 and 1. Whereas other numeration systems are interesting in themselves, they have only marginal utility in the real world. On the other hand, the base-two, or *binary* system, has a use that is central to the technology of our modern world; the binary system is the numeration system of our giant computing machines.

The binary system was the invention of Gottfried Leibniz, the seventeenth-century mathematician who was the co-inventor, with Isaac Newton, of the calculus. Leibniz saw the world as consisting of God, whom he represented by the numeral 1, and the void, which he represented by 0. With the digits 1 and 0 Leibniz could represent any number, just as he felt God could create the universe from the void. For more than two hundred years, the binary system remained a mathematical curiosity, until it became essential for computer science.

In the binary system, the base is two, so grouping is done on the basis of two to a group. Thus it is obvious that there would be many groups of two, even in fairly small numbers. Hence binary numerals tend to have many digits.

Here is how grouping in twos gives us binary numerals:

Base-ten numerals	Binary grouping	Binary numeral	Suggested number names*
1	X	1	one
2	XX	10_{two}	twin
3	XX X	11_{two}	twin one
4	XX XX	100_{two}	one twindred
5	XX X XX	101_{two}	one twindred one

* This set of names was suggested by a pupil studying binary numerals.

6		110_{two}	one twindred twin
7		111_{two}	one twindred twin one
8		1000_{two}	one twosand
9		1001_{two}	one twosand one
10		1010_{two}	one twosand twin

One way to keep place value straight in base two is to use book-keeper columns.

Base-ten numeral	*two × two × two × two* (*sixteens*)	*two × two × two* (*eights*)	*two × two* (*fours*)	*twos*	*ones*
11		1	1	0	1
23	1	0	1	1	1
30	1	1	1	1	0

We get into five-place numerals as early as 16_{ten} (10000_{two}); even so small a number as 63_{ten} has six places (111111_{two}).

Despite the tendency of binary numerals to swell rapidly, the binary system would be ideal for youngsters who have difficulty memorizing basic addition and multiplication facts. There are only three possible addition and multiplication facts to be learned:

$$0 + 0 = 0 \qquad 0 \times 0 = 0$$
$$1 + 0 = 1 \qquad 1 \times 0 = 0$$
$$1 + 1 = 10 \qquad 1 \times 1 = 1$$

With only two symbols to the system, one can pair them in convenient either-or situations. This is like an electric switch which is either "on" or "off." If it is off, assign a 0 value to it; if it is on, assign a 1 value to it. Set up a panel of lights, and, if the lights are properly arranged, virtually any number can be represented in binary numerals by lamps in an "on" or "off" position. For example, if four lights were in the on–on–off–off position, the numeral 1100_{two} would be displayed.

We do not wish to be sidetracked into computer mathematics, but simply hope to establish the connection between some ideas in number-base concepts and their application to an increasingly important aspect of our computer-oriented world. Few youngsters who study base 5, 12, and 2 numerals will probably ever serve as computer mathematicians or programmers, but by developing an understanding of how these machines operate they are more likely to feel at home in a world in which many routine thinking tasks will be performed by these machines.

One of the by-products of the study of various numeration systems is a better, richer understanding of the concept of number, as contrasted with numeral. A student must see very soon in his work with various bases that the number twelve, for example, can be represented normally as

$$12 \qquad \frac{24}{2} \qquad 6 \times 2 \qquad 8 + 4$$

but also, in an entirely different dimension, as

$$10_{twelve} \qquad 22_{five} \qquad 14_{eight} \qquad 1100_{two}$$

At appropriate levels, certain general aspects of numeration systems are explored. The teacher raises the question whether in any or all of these bases the fundamental properties of the operations of arithmetic (commutative, associative, distributive) might be expected to hold true. Before the operation of the properties is tested, the students are invited to speculate on whether they operate and why. If some students are uncertain, they will be invited to try the properties out in various numeration systems, and the results might resemble the following:

> *Commutative Property for Addition:* $(a + b = b + a)$
> Base ten
> $5 + 7 = 7 + 5 = 12$
> Base five
> $11_{five} + 4 = 4 + 11_{five} = 20_{five}$

Base twelve

$X_{twelve} + E_{twelve} = E_{twelve} + X_{twelve} = 19_{twelve}$

Base two

$10_{two} + 101_{two} = 101_{two} + 10_{two} = 111_{two}$

Commutative Property for Multiplication: $(a \times b = b \times a)$

Base ten

$2 \times 3 = 3 \times 2 = 6$

Base five

$12_{five} \times 3 = 3 \times 12_{five} = 41_{five}$

Base twelve

$16_{twelve} \times 5 = 5 \times 16_{twelve} = 76_{twelve}$

Base two

$101_{two} \times 1101_{two} = 1101_{two} \times 101_{two} = 100000_{two}$

Similar examples can be tried to check the associative and distributive properties.

We have noted earlier that the new mathematics programs aim to foster creativity in mathematics. The topic of numeration systems offers an excellent opportunity in this respect. Even average students respond to the challenge to build a numeration system to a base not studied in class. Some students are encouraged to set up a base-twenty system, after the Mayans, but using conventional numeration, which was not available to the Mayans. Students are asked to build their own number systems, using, not conventional numerals, but symbols such as □, △, ○, and to operate in this system. For some students being asked to develop a numeration system that does not depend on place value is a particularly challenging assignment.

EXERCISES

1. Which of the following statements are true?
   a. No matter what the number base, $10 \times 10 = 100$.
   b. The larger the number base the fewer digits needed in numerals for large numbers.
   c. Numerals for even counting numbers always have an even digit in the last place on the right.
   d. Numbers divisible by the number base have numerals which end in zero.
   e. The fraction $\frac{2}{3}$ represents the same number in base five as in base ten.

2. Change these numerals to base-ten numerals for representing the
   same number.
   a. 43_{five}
   b. 10101_{two}
   c. 43_{twelve}
   d. 100_{seven}
   e. 1210_{four}

3. Express the numbers of these base-ten numerals with numerals in
   the indicated base.
   a. 18 in base five
   b. 32 in base twelve
   c. 15 in base two
   d. 27 in base four
   e. 183 in base five

4. Compute as indicated with these base-five numerals. Leave the
   answers in base five. Check your work by converting to base-ten
   numerals.

   a. $\begin{array}{r} 32_{\text{five}} \\ +43_{\text{five}} \\ \hline \end{array}$ b. $\begin{array}{r} 403_{\text{five}} \\ -32_{\text{five}} \\ \hline \end{array}$ c. $\begin{array}{r} 231_{\text{five}} \\ \times 3 \\ \hline \end{array}$ d. $\begin{array}{r} 324_{\text{five}} \\ \times 24_{\text{five}} \\ \hline \end{array}$ e. $323_{\text{five}} \div 4$

5. Compute as indicated with these binary numerals.

   a. $\begin{array}{r} 1011 \\ +101 \\ \hline \end{array}$ b. $\begin{array}{r} 1101 \\ -11 \\ \hline \end{array}$ c. $\begin{array}{r} 111 \\ \times 10 \\ \hline \end{array}$ d. $\begin{array}{r} 10110 \\ \times 11 \\ \hline \end{array}$ e. $111101 \div 11$

6. Compute as indicated with these base-six numerals.

   a. $\begin{array}{r} 45_{\text{six}} \\ +32_{\text{six}} \\ \hline \end{array}$ b. $\begin{array}{r} 304_{\text{six}} \\ +54_{\text{six}} \\ \hline \end{array}$ c. $\begin{array}{r} 213_{\text{six}} \\ -42_{\text{six}} \\ \hline \end{array}$ d. $\begin{array}{r} 23_{\text{six}} \\ \times 4 \\ \hline \end{array}$ e. $324_{\text{six}} \div 4$

7. Make a new base-four numeration system using these symbols for
   digits: $0 = \cdot$, $1 = /$, $2 = >$, $3 = \triangle$.
   a. Use these digits to write numerals for numbers from one through
      sixteen.
   b. Show by grouping dots what $/\triangle>$ represents.
   c. Change $>\triangle>$ to a base-ten numeral.
   d. What is the largest number that can be represented by a three-
      digit number in this system?
   e. Develop the addition table for this system.

FINITE NUMBER SYSTEMS

7

Earlier, in our discussion of bases and numeration systems, we showed how 2 and 4 could be added and the answer expressed as 11. (You will recognize, of course, that this answer indicates that the numerals are in base five.)

There is yet another mathematical situation that yields seemingly odd results when two numbers are added. Consider these additions:

$$6 + 4 = 10$$
$$7 + 5 = 12$$
$$8 + 6 = 2$$
$$9 + 7 = 4$$
$$12 + 5 = 5$$

The first two additions appear quite "normal." But what are we to make of the last three additions? The answers appear to defy common sense. Yet, do they really? Suppose that each of the above numbers represents an hour of the day on our regular twelve-hour clock. Is it not true that 6 hours after 8 o'clock is 2 o'clock; that 7 hours after 9 o'clock is 4 o'clock; that 5 hours after 12 o'clock is 5 o'clock?

Actually, when we add these clock numbers, we count around the dial in a clockwise direction. Our results are related to addition and subtraction as follows.

First $8 + 6 = 14$. Then $14 - 12 = 2$.

a. $\begin{array}{r} 8 \\ +6 \\ \hline 14 \end{array}$ $\begin{array}{r} 14 \\ -12 \\ \hline 2 \end{array}$ b. $\begin{array}{r} 9 \\ +7 \\ \hline 16 \end{array}$ $\begin{array}{r} 16 \\ -12 \\ \hline 4 \end{array}$ c. $\begin{array}{r} 12 \\ +5 \\ \hline 17 \end{array}$ $\begin{array}{r} 17 \\ -12 \\ \hline 5 \end{array}$

In other words, with 12 as a kind of "base," our answers—2, 4, 5—are the *remainders* after the subtraction of a twelve. In this kind of arithmetic, we call 12 the *modulus* of our numbers. We have used 12 as a modulus to obtain the remainders we have shown. When 12 is the modulus, we have a kind of arithmetic which we identify to youngsters as "clock arithmetic"—for obvious reasons. More formally, this kind of arithmetic is called *modular arithmetic*, and any number (except 1 and 0) can serve as a modulus.

But let us explore clock arithmetic a little further. You know that the Armed Services use, not the 12-hour clock, but the 24-hour clock. Let us try to translate the hours on this 24-hour clock into hours on the 12-hour clock.

24-hour clock	1	2	3	4	5	6	7	8	9	10	11	12	13	14	15
													-12	-12	-12
12-hour clock	1	2	3	4	5	6	7	8	9	10	11	12	1	2	3

24-hour clock	16	17	18	19	20	21	22	23	24
	-12	-12	-12	-12	-12	-12	-12	-12	-12
12-hour clock	4	5	6	7	8	9	10	11	12

If we examine our 12-hour counterparts of the 24-hour clock, we find that we have two cycles of numbers from 1 to 12. If we should somewhere find a clock with 36 hours, we would find that the 36 numbers would still translate into the same 12 numbers of our standard clock. Just to show this with one number:

36-hour clock	35		23
	-12		-12
24-hour clock	23	12-hour clock	11

What we have done, then, is to establish a special little number system with only 12 elements. Mathematicians call a number system with a limited number of elements a *finite* number system. This is in contrast with our standard number system, which we call "infinite" because the number of elements is endless.

We have been discussing a modulo-12 number system (called mod 12 for short) because we are familiar with the 12-hour clock. But finite number systems are not limited to mod 12. We may use any number as a modulus. To translate numbers in our infinite system to numbers in any finite system, we simply subtract the modulus a sufficient number of times (or divide by the modulus) until we get the modular number in that finite system. This modular number is the remainder after the subtraction or division by the modulus.

The results below tell us how to convert numbers from base-10 numerals to modular numbers.

1. Change 25 to a mod-8 number.

$$25 \div 8 = 3 \text{ remainder } 1$$
$$25 = 1 \text{ (mod 8)}$$

2. Change 17 to a mod-3 number.

$$17 \div 3 = 5 \text{ remainder } 2$$
$$17 = 2 \text{ (mod 3)}$$

3. Change 9 to a mod-5 number.

$$9 \div 5 = 1 \text{ remainder } 4$$
$$9 = 4 \text{ (mod 5)}$$

4. Change 67 to a mod-4 number.

$$67 \div 4 = 16 \text{ remainder } 3$$
$$67 = 3 \text{ (mod 4)}$$

Since a modular system consists of remainders, after subtraction or division by the modulus base, the number of elements in that system will equal the number in the modulus base. A mod-5 system will have 5 numbers. A mod-8 system will have 8 numbers.

ADDITION IN MODULAR ARITHMETIC

As we might suspect, operations can be performed in these number systems, and it is not surprising to find that youngsters are intrigued with the "queer" results that they obtain. Here are some additions in modular-5 and mod-8 systems:

Modulus 5

$1 + 3 = 4$
$2 + 2 = 4$
$2 + 4 = 1 \text{ (mod 5) since } 6 - 5 = 1 \text{ (or } 6 \div 5 = 1 \text{ remainder 1)}$
$4 + 4 = 3 \text{ (mod 5) since } 8 - 5 = 3$

Modulus 8

$3 + 4 = 7$
$3 + 7 = 2 \pmod 8$ since $10 - 8 = 2$ (or $10 \div 8 = 1$ remainder 2)
$7 + 4 = 3 \pmod 8$ since $11 - 8 = 3$
$7 + 7 = 6 \pmod 8$ since $14 - 8 = 6$

When clock numbers and finite number systems were first introduced into the new mathematics programs, emphasis was placed on their appeal as curiosities. However, in the past few years less attention has been paid to this aspect of these systems and more to the opportunities they provide for a study of them as *mathematical systems*, with their own properties. Some of these properties are quite similar to those of our own system; others are significantly different. Let us examine in some detail one such system—the mod-5 system. It will be useful to set out the elements in this system in clock fashion, as we do with our regular clock (mod 12) numbers.

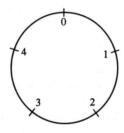

Notice that, unlike our regular 12-hr clock, our mod-5 clock has a 0 in the position between 4 and 1. It would not have been incorrect for us to have a 5 in this position, but there are two reasons for preferring the 0 to the 5. First, we must recall that mod numbers are remainders. If 5 is an element in the mod-5 set, we can perform the subtraction $5 - 5$ and obtain 0 as one of our elements. Second, since we have a 0 in our everyday number system, it will be convenient also to have a 0 in our mod-5 system. This will also suggest that a mod-5 system is somewhat related to the base-five numeration system.

In short, then, our mod-5 system consists of these five numbers: 0, 1, 2, 3, 4. We can, of course, "add" in this system. This "addition" is not quite the same as addition with counting numbers but we will not worry about that distinction in this chapter.

We have already seen that $2 + 4 = 1 \pmod 5$ since $2 + 4 = 6$ and $(6 - 5) = 1$. By using the mod-5 clock we eliminate the need

to perform the intermediate subtraction of 5. To illustrate the sum
2 + 4 on the clock, we start with 2, move 4 places in a clockwise
direction, and arrive at 1, our sum (see illustration below). To add
4 + 4, we start with 4, move 4 places in a clockwise direction, and
arrive at our sum, 3.

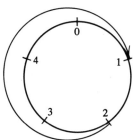

There is no need for us (or youngsters) to memorize all the addition
combinations in the mod-5 system, but we will want to study certain
patterns of the combinations. So we construct an addition table in the
system to get all the addition combinations as follows:

Addition Table (Mod 5)

+	0	1	2	3	4
0	0	1	2	3	4
1	1	2	3	4	0
2	2	3	4	0	1
3	3	4	0	1	2
4	4	0	1	2	3

We notice immediately that the sum of every addition combination
is a number that is one of the 5 numbers in our system. In other words,
the mod-5 system is closed for the addition operation. You will recall
that our everyday counting number system is also closed with respect
to addition. The sum of two counting numbers is always another
unique counting number.

We know that our counting number system is commutative with
respect to addition; that is, for example, 21 + 16 = 16 + 21. Is

the mod-5 system also commutative for addition? Is $4 + 3 = 3 + 4$? Is $2 + 1 = 1 + 2$? From our table, we see that $4 + 3 = 2$ (mod 5) and that $3 + 4 = 2$ (mod 5); that $2 + 1 = 3$ and that $1 + 2 = 3$. For any pair of mod-5 numbers that we choose, the order in which we add them would not affect their sum. So we may say, for our second property of the mod-5 system, that addition is commutative.

You will recall that in our everyday number system, addition is associative; that is, we may add a group of numbers like $4 + 9 + 7$ either by combining 4 and 9 and then adding the sum, 13, to 7, or by adding 4 to the sum of 9 and 7.

Is our mod-5 system associative with respect to addition? Let us test it with this addition:

$$\text{Does } (2 + 3) + 4 = 2 + (3 + 4)?$$
$$2 + 3 = 0 \text{ (mod 5)}$$
$$\text{and} \quad 0 + 4 = 4$$
$$\text{Hence} \quad (2 + 3) + 4 = 0 + 4 = 4$$

$$3 + 4 = 2 \text{ (mod 5)}$$
$$\text{and} \quad 2 + 2 = 4$$
$$\text{Hence} \quad 2 + (3 + 4) = 2 + 2 = 4$$

The sum is the same in both instances, so we may say, for our third property, that addition in mod 5 is associative.

Our modular system has a fourth property which is also found in our everyday number system. In everyday arithmetic there is one number which when added to another number yields the first number as a sum.

$$12 + 0 = 12$$
$$9 + 0 = 9$$

Zero in this case is called an *identity number*, or, *element* because it yields the identical number we start with. In the mod-5 system, 0 also performs this function.

$$3 + 0 = 3$$
$$4 + 0 = 4$$

Another interesting addition property was noted in the set of integers. For every integer there is another number which, when added to the first number, in effect "undoes" the addition. Look at these pairs of integers:

$$^+3 + \ ^-3 = 0$$
$$^+16 + \ ^-16 = 0$$

Each of the positive numbers, $^+3$ and $^+16$, has a kind of twin which nullifies the addition. For each of these pairs of integers one is a positive number; the other is negative. We say that one is the *additive inverse* of the other.

We know that none of our mod-5 numbers is negative. Nevertheless, is it possible that we can find pairs of numbers which will undo each other when added—which, in effect, will add up to 0?

Let us look closely at our addition table. When we examine the horizontal rows of numbers and their sums, we see 0 as a sum several times. In the 1 row, for example, we see 0 as a sum in the position in the 4 column. This means that when 4 and 1 are added the sum is 0.

$$4 + 1 = 0$$

Similarly, there is a 0 in the 2 row in the 3 column, a 0 in the 3 row in the 2 column, and a 0 in the 4 row in the 1 column. So we have two pairs of numbers that are additive inverses.

$$\begin{cases} 1 + 4 = 0 \\ 4 + 1 = 0 \end{cases}$$
$$\begin{cases} 2 + 3 = 0 \\ 3 + 2 = 0 \end{cases}$$

Notice that if these numbers were integers, their sums in counting numbers would be 5. But 5 in mod-5 arithmetic is an analog of 0, so we can see that each system—integers and mod 5—is consistent within itself and related to the other through this additive inverse property.

We have seen that our mod-5 system and our integer number system have the following similarities, even though each system gives us quite different kinds of answers to addition of its elements:

1. The set of mod-5 numbers is closed with respect to addition.
2. The set of mod-5 numbers is commutative with respect to addition.

Mod 5 $2 + 3 = 3 + 2 = 0$

Integers $2 + 3 = 3 + 2 = 5$

3. The set of mod-5 numbers is associative with respect to addition.

Mod 5 $\qquad$ $2 + (3 + 4) = (2 + 3) + 4 = 4$

Integers $\qquad$ $2 + (3 + 4) = (2 + 3) + 4 = 9$

4. The set of mod-5 numbers has an identity element with respect to addition.

Mod 5 $\qquad$ $3 + 0 = 3$

Integers $\qquad$ $3 + 0 = 3$

5. Each member of the set of mod-5 numbers has an additive inverse.

Mod 5 $\qquad$ $3 + 2 = 0$

Integers $\qquad$ $^+3 + {}^-3 = 0$

As we know from the last chapter, whenever a set of elements and an operation on these elements has the properties numbered 1, 3, 4, and 5 above, it is called a mathematical *group*. Hence, the set of mod-5 numbers and the addition operation are an example of a mathematical structure called a *group*.

MULTIPLICATION IN MODULAR ARITHMETIC

You probably had little difficulty understanding how we add modular numbers. But you may wonder whether we can multiply modular numbers, and how. With integers when we see a statement like

$$2 \times 3 = ?$$

almost instinctively we reply, "6." But how shall we respond when we are confronted with

$$2 \times 3 = ?$$

in mod-5 arithmetic?

Let us first agree that it *is* possible to multiply in modular arithmetic. We can understand this quite readily if we think of multiplication as a kind of condensed, or shorthand, addition. When we say multiply 2×3 we are really saying, "Add two 3's," like this:

$$3 + 3 = 6$$

On a number line, we can show this addition even more clearly:

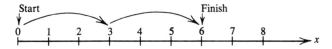

Starting at 0, we take 2 jumps of 3 units each.

Looking at multiplication this way, we can, perhaps, think more clearly about multiplication in the mod-5 system. First, let us do the multiplication 2×3 by adding two 3's in mod 5.

$$3 + 3 = ? \ (\text{mod } 5)$$

We know from our addition table that the answer to this addition problem is 1 (mod 5). So

$$3 + 3 = 1 \ (\text{mod } 5)$$

and, therefore,

$$2 \times 3 = 1 \ (\text{mod } 5)$$

Now let us show this on our mod-5 "clock."

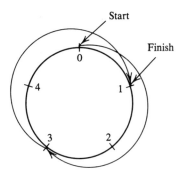

Starting at 0, we take 1 turn of 3 units and land at 3. Then we take a second turn of 3 units and land at 1. Once again, in mod 5,

$$2 \times 3 = 1 \ (\text{mod } 5)$$

By using either the addition method or "turn-around-the-clock" method, we can find the product of any two elements in the mod-5 system. In fact, we can build up a complete table for mod-5 multiplication. Here it is:

Multiplication Table (Mod 5)

×	0	1	2	3	4
0	0	0	0	0	0
1	0	1	2	3	4
2	0	2	4	1	3
3	0	3	1	4	2
4	0	4	3	2	1

Youngsters who study mod-5 arithmetic are not, of course, obliged to memorize the multiplication table, as they do with the standard arithmetic multiplication table. Rather, it is available to them for use in performing individual multiplications.

As with mod-5 addition, the true significance of studying mod-5 multiplication lies not in performing this operation itself but rather in studying the properties of multiplication. We shall not take the time to develop these properties in detail, as we did with the properties of addition. Instead we shall present them in summary form. Test the following properties with the mod-5 multiplication table or a mod-5 clock.

1. The set of mod-5 numbers is closed with respect to multiplication.

2. The set of mod-5 numbers is commutative with respect to multiplication.

   Mod-5 Arithmetic $2 \times 3 = 3 \times 2 = 1 \pmod 5$

   Standard Arithmetic $2 \times 3 = 3 \times 2 = 6$

3. The set of mod-5 numbers is associative with respect to multiplication.

   Mod-5 Arithmetic $2 \times (3 \times 4) = (2 \times 3) \times 4 = 4$
   $\pmod 5$

   Standard Arithmetic $2 \times (3 \times 4) = (2 \times 3) \times 4 = 24$

4. The set of mod-5 numbers is distributive with respect to multiplication over addition.

   Mod-5 Arithmetic $2 \times (3 + 4) = (2 \times 3) + (2 \times 4) = 4$
                                                    (mod 5)

   Standard Arithmetic $2 \times (3 + 4) = (2 \times 3) + (2 + 4) = 14$

5. The set of mod-5 numbers has an identity element with respect to multiplication.

   Mod-5 Arithmetic $4 \times 1 = 4$
   Standard Arithmetic $4 \times 1 = 4$

6. Each number of the set of mod-5 numbers has a multiplicative inverse.

   Mod-5 Arithmetic $4 \times 4 = 1 \pmod 5$
                                 $3 \times 2 = 1 \pmod 5$
                                 $2 \times 3 = 1 \pmod 5$
                                 $1 \times 1 = 1 \pmod 5$

   Standard Arithmetic $4 \times \frac{1}{4} = 1$

We see that, as was the case with addition, mod-5 multiplication has much in common with multiplication in standard arithmetic. These six properties, plus the five properties of addition, tell us that the structure of the mod-5 system under multiplication and addition is such that it can be classified as a mathematical *field;* so too the positive and negative numbers of algebra (excluding zero) under the addition and multiplication operations form a mathematical field. The similarities between the two systems are really quite remarkable, especially when we consider that one system consists of a set of only five elements and the other consists of an infinity of elements. If we were to go on to examine subtraction and division with mod 5—which we shall not take the time to do—we would find additional similarities between the two systems, as well as some interesting differences.

At this point, you may well wonder whether the study of modular arithmetic by youngsters is worth the time spent on it. After all, you may claim, modular arithmetic has no practical value. One cannot use it either in building a bridge or in computing one's income tax. As we have attempted to point out before in this book, not all of mathematics has an immediate application. At one time the test of whether any part of mathematics was to be taught was its usefulness in real life.

Modern mathematics says that usefulness should be only one criterion for the study of a particular topic. A great deal of mathematics that has no practical application is of intense interest because of what it reveals about the nature of mathematics.

And this is precisely the case with modular arithmetic. It opens a pupil's eyes to the fact that a number system which on the surface appears to be so bizarre, can, on closer inspection, have many of the very same characteristics as the system that he deals with in everyday life. In a sense, this is the same kind of conclusion that a biology student interested in human physiology will come to about the value of studying the structure of an embryo pig. Yet, few persons will condemn the study of the embryo pig because it is not "practical" for anyone except the would-be biologist or physician.

Besides, the modern curriculum maker would ask, when is one to say whether a topic is practical or not? Today, modular arithmetic is useful only to the professional mathematician and scientist. But who knows how it will be used in the future? One recalls the fact that in 1858 the British mathematician Arthur Cayley invented a kind of algebra called matrix algebra. Matrix algebra had slight interest even to mathematicians for three-quarters of a century (even though it is one of the few mathematical systems in which multiplication is not commutative). Had matrix algebra been taught to high school students in Cayley's time (he died in 1895) their parents could rightly have claimed that their youngsters were learning a subject that was not practical. However, today matrix algebra *is* being taught in high schools, but complaining parents would no longer be right about the usefulness of the topic. For, within the past quarter of a century, matrix algebra has found an important role in quantum mechanics, atomic physics, and statistical research, roles that not even Cayley dreamed it might some day have.

EXERCISES

1. Convert these integers to mod-5 numbers.
   a. 13   d. 46
   b. 19   e. 25
   c. 32
2. Find three integers which could convert to these modular numbers.
   a. 2 (mod 5)   d. 4 (mod 7)
   b. 3 (mod 7)   e. 9 (mod 12)
   c. 5 (mod 6)

3. Make up an addition table for a mod-7 system and use it to find x.

   a. $5 + 6 = x$ (mod 7)   d. $x + 6 = 6$ (mod 7)

   b. $x + 3 = 2$ (mod 7)   e. Find x if x is the additive in-

   c. $x + 4 = 0$ (mod 7)   verse for 5 (mod 7).

4. Make up a multiplication table for a mod-6 system. Consider 1 as the identity element with respect to multiplication.

   a. What is the inverse of 5 with respect to multiplication? Find x if $5x = 1$ (mod 6).

   b. What is the inverse of 2 with respect to multiplication? Find x if $2x = 1$ (mod 6).

   c. Find x if $3x = 0$ (mod 6).

   d. Find x if $4x = 2$ (mod 6).

   e. Why is the set of mod-6 numbers with respect to the multiplication operation not a mathematical group?

5. Suppose that we have a finite arithmetic made up of the set of $R = \{0, E\}$ and the operation $\oplus$. Consider E and 0 to refer to even and odd numbers and $\oplus$ to be addition. The table for this operation is as follows:

$\oplus$	0	E
0	E	0
E	0	E

   a. Is set R closed with respect to $\oplus$?

   b. Is set R commutative with respect to $\oplus$?

   c. Is set R associative with respect to $\oplus$?

   d. Since $0 + E = 0$ and $E + E = E$, what is the identity element for addition?

   e. Since $0 + 0 = E$ and $E + E = E$, what is the inverse of 0 with respect to $\oplus$?

6. Suppose that you have a set of three elements $S = \{a, b, c\}$ and an operation *. Make up a table for this operation and check it to see if it has the properties of a group.

EQUATIONS, PROBABILITY, AND
LINEAR PROGRAMMING

8

In order to communicate with others, we have to use words and sentences. Words are symbols for ideas and objects. Thus, we use the word "dog" to identify a certain animal. We could just as well have used the word "xuz" for this animal. But once we have decided to use "dog" or "xuz," we know what is meant by "dog" or "xuz."

In mathematics we use words to identify ideas—ideas such as "three" or "addition" or "is equal to." However, in mathematics it is usually more efficient to use symbols than words. Thus, we use symbols such as "3" for a number, "+" for the addition operation, and "=" for a kind of comparison.

When we express ideas in everyday conversation, we use sentences. The sentence "Washington is the capital of the United States" is a true statement. If we say "San Francisco is the largest city in the United States," we have a false statement. If we say "He is the senator from Illinois," we do not know whether the sentence is true or false. To decide whether the sentence is true or false, we must know who is referred to by the pronoun "he." Sentences whose truth or falsity is unknown are called *open sentences*. When a sentence can be identified as true or false, it is called a *statement*. Of course, we assume that a sentence cannot be both true and false at the same time.

Much of our everyday conversation is about quality rather than quantity. We may describe things as being beautiful, rough, green, soft, sweet, or pleasant. In mathematical conversation, we usually describe things in terms of shape, size, location, order, or time. Often we use numbers as measures of how many, how much, when, and where.

We express quantitative ideas in sentences just as we express other ideas in sentences. The difference is that in mathematics we write our sentences in symbols. Here are some true sentences from arithmetic.

$$3 + 4 = 7 \qquad 3 \times 4 = 12$$
$$^+5 - {}^-3 = {}^+8 \qquad \tfrac{3}{4} = 0.75$$

If we translate these sentences into words, we have the following statements:

The sum of three and four is seven.

The product of three multiplied by four is twelve.

The difference between positive five and negative three is positive eight.

The quotient of 3 divided by 4 is the same as the quotient of 75 divided by 100.

Note that each of the sentences above uses the equality symbol, "=." This symbol "=" represents the verb "is" or "equals." Mathematics usually uses equality to indicate that we have two numerals for the same number. Thus, if we say that $3 + 4 = 7$, we are saying that "$3 + 4$" and "7" are names or numerals for the same number. Likewise "$^+5 - {}^-3$" is a numeral for "$^+8$," "3×4" is a numeral for "12," and "$\frac{3}{4}$" and "0.75" are numerals for the same number.

In a similar way, the English sentence, "Washington is the capital of the United States," can be written:

$$\text{Washington} = \text{the capital of the United States}$$

Then, "Washington" and "the capital of the United States" are names of the same city.

Sometimes we may wish to say that two numerals do *not* represent the same number. To do so, we may use these symbols:

$$\neq \text{ "not equal"}$$
$$\text{or } < \text{ "less than"}$$
$$\text{or } > \text{ "greater than"}$$

To say $3 + 4$ is not equal to 8, we write the sentence: $3 + 4 \neq 8$. This says that "$3 + 4$" is not another numeral for "8."

$3 + 4 < 8$ says $3 + 4$ is less than 8.

$3 + 4 > 8$ says $3 + 4$ is greater than 8.

$3 + 4 = 8$ says $3 + 4$ is another numeral for 8.

The last two sentences, $3 + 4 > 8$ and $3 + 4 = 8$ are, of course, false statements.

Sentences which express an equality such as $3 + 4 = 7$ or $3 + 4 = 8$ are called *equations*. An equation is a sentence about equality.

Equations may be true or false. Sentences which indicate that two numerals do not represent the same number are called *inequalities*. (One reform group, the Illinois Committee, has called them *inequations*, but we shall use the more common term, inequalities.) Inequalities may also be true or false, as, for example, $3 + 4 > 5$ and $7 + 4 < 9$.

OPEN SENTENCES

One of the most useful sentences in mathematics is the *open sentence*. An open sentence is one which may be either true or false. Thus "three times some number is 45" is an open sentence; it may be either true or false, depending on what "some number" stands for. In symbols we may write this open sentence as: $3 \times \square = 45$ or $3n = 45$. Here the symbols $\square$ or n are used to represent some numeral. The symbols $\square$ and n are usually called *variables*. However, the Illinois Committee calls them "pronumerals," since they correspond to pronouns in open English sentences.

If $\square$ is replaced by 7 in the sentence, $3 \times \square = 45$, then we obtain a false statement; namely, $3 \times 7 = 45$. If $\square$ (or n) is replaced by 15, we obtain a true statement. Usually we are searching for the numeral which will make the equation a true statement. We say $\{15\}$ is the *truth set* or *solution set* for the equation $3 \times \square = 45$ (or $3n = 45$). Traditionally we have called 15 the *root* of the equation.

We may use open sentences in everyday language, too. For example, "Boston is in the state of ⬚⬚⬚⬚⬚⬚⬚." If we replace our variable with Maine, we have a false statement. The truth set for this open sentence is {Massachusetts}.

What are the possible replacements for our variable in this sentence? It appears to be the set of names for the states of the United States. This set of possible replacements is called the *domain* of our open sentence.

For the open sentence $3n = 45$, we could consider the domain to be the set of counting numbers, $\{1, 2, 3, 4 \ldots\}$.

Consider the open sentence "＿＿＿ is a vowel." The truth set for this sentence is $\{a, e, i, o, u\}$. What is the domain of the variable? It would appear to be the set of letters of our alphabet.

Suppose we have the open sentence $3n = 5$. If the domain is the counting numbers, the truth set is the empty set, for there is no counting number which, when multiplied by 3, equals 5. If $3n = 5$, then $n = 5 \div 3$. But the quotient $5 \div 3$ is not a counting number. On the other hand, if we say that our domain is the set of rational numbers (the numbers that can be expressed as fractions, such as $\frac{1}{2}$, $\frac{2}{3}$, and $1\frac{4}{5}$), then our truth set is $\{\frac{5}{3}\}$ or $\{1\frac{2}{3}\}$.

In elementary arithmetic it was customary to write open sentences as:

$$7 + 5 = \underline{\quad} \quad \text{or} \quad 7 + 5 = ?$$
$$8 + ? = 15 \quad \text{or} \quad 9 \times 8 = ?$$

The new arithmetic usually uses symbols such as $\square$, $\triangle$, or $\bigcirc$, called *frames*, as placeholders for the unknown numbers. It seems that it is easy for children to visualize or try out various numbers in the frames in searching for the truth set for equations. Then open sentences such as the following provide a setting for discovering number relations and practicing computation:

Addition

$6 + 5 = \square$

$7 + \triangle = 19$

$\square + \square + 3 = 11$

Subtraction

$12 - 7 = \square$

$13 - \triangle = 6$

$(\square + 4) - 4 = 8$

Multiplication

$7 \times 8 = \square$

$6 \times \triangle = 42$

$2 \times (\square + 5) = 36$

Division

$30 \div 5 = \square$

$\triangle \div 8 = 9$

$(\square + 9) \div 3 = 6$

Open sentences can also be used to discover properties of one and zero:

$5 \times \square = 5 \qquad \square \times 1 = \square \qquad \dfrac{8}{8} = \square \qquad \dfrac{\square}{\square} = 1 (\square \neq 0)$

$\dfrac{7}{\square} = 7 \qquad 4 + \square = 4 \qquad \triangle \times 0 = 0 \qquad 6 \times \triangle = 0$

$\dfrac{\triangle}{9} = 0 \qquad \dfrac{0}{n} = 0$

In using frames as variables, we have two rules to follow. If the frames in a problem are the same, we *must* use the same numeral as a replacement for each. If the frames are different, we *may* use the same numeral *or* different numerals as replacements. Then open sentences can be used to discover the properties of addition and multiplication.

Use different replacements for the □ and △ in these open sentences.

1. □ + △ = △ + □
2. □ × △ = △ × □
3. (□ + △) + 7 = □ + (△ + 7)
4. (□ × △) × 3 = □ × (△ × 3)
5. □ × (△ + 5) = (□ × △) + (□ × 5)

No matter what numerals are used as replacements for the frames in each sentence above, the equality is true. This suggests that they express rules or properties. You will recognize these properties as the *commutative*, *associative*, and *distributive* properties of addition and multiplication.

When letters, rather than frames, are used as variables, the sentences above are:

1. $a + b = b + a$
2. $a \times b = b \times a$
3. $(a + b) + c = a + (b + c)$
4. $(a \times b) \times c = a \times (b \times c)$
5. $a \times (b + c) = (a \times b) + (a \times c)$

Open sentences with frames for variables can also be used to discover identities and inverses:

Identity element   1. 2 + □ = 2   2. △ + □ = △
                         3. 3 × △ = 3   4. □ × △ = □

Thus, the identity for addition is zero, and for multiplication it is one.

Inverse element   5. 2 + □ = 0   6. △ + □ = 0
                         7. 3 × △ = 1   8. □ × △ = 1

The additive inverse for 2 is $^{-}2$, and the multiplicative inverse for 3 is $\frac{1}{3}$.

Open sentences such as □ + △ = △ + □ are called *identities*. They are true for any replacements from the domain of the variable. An open sentence such as □ + 3 = 8 is true only if □ = 5. Open sentences which are true only for certain members of the replacement set are called *conditional* equations.

We have already seen that some open sentences have no replacement for the frame which will make it a true sentence. If our replacement set is the counting numbers (the domain of □ is the set of counting numbers), what is the truth set for this open sentence:

$$\square + 7 = 5$$

The truth set is the empty set, $\square = \varnothing$ or $\square = \{\ \}$, since no counting number added to 7 will give 5 as a sum.

However, if the domain of □ is the set of integers, then $\square = \{^{-}2\}$ is the truth set.

When the open sentence is an inequality, the truth set often has several members. If the domain of each variable is the counting numbers, here are the truth sets for these sentences.

1. $\square + 2 < 7$: $\square = \{1, 2, 3, 4\}$
2. $\triangle - 5 > 8$: $\triangle = \{14, 15, 16, \ldots\}$
3. $3 \times \square < 12$: $\square = \{1, 2, 3\}$

We have said that open sentences are widely used in elementary school. They are graded by complexity; here are the types of sentences used at different grade levels in many of the new programs:

Grade	Example	
1	$3 + \square = 7$	$5 - \square = 1$
2, 3	$\square + \square + 3 = 11$	$\square + \square + \square = 1$
4, 5	$(3 \times \square) + \triangle = 14$	$\square + \triangle = 10$
6, 7	$(\square \times \square) + (2 \times \square) = 15$	$3n - 7 = 14$
8, 9	$3x + 19 = 4 - 2x$	$x^2 - 5x + 4 = 0$

As the pupil becomes more mature, letters are used consistently as variables, and the equations become more complex.

$$n + 5 = 14 \qquad 2n - 3 = 27$$
$$x + y = 15 \qquad y = 3x + 7$$
$$2x - 5 = 17 \qquad x > y^2$$

In finding the truth sets for these sentences, the pupils are not given rules. Rather they are encouraged to estimate, explore, try out various methods. Sometimes the problems are solved by the number line.

□ + □ + 4 = 10

Some students may discover shortcuts: If □ + □ + 4 = 10, then □ + □ = 6 and □ = 3.

After many experiences the pupils find and remember a variety of number relations. These sentences with frames then become one way of practicing computational skills. Having students make their own frame sentences adds interest and understanding. Sometimes these original sentences turn up sentences such as □ × □ = 5. The truth set here is the empty set if the replacement set for □ is the set of rational numbers. In an inequality such as 3 × □ > 13, the question may arise as to the numeral for the smallest number which can be used as a replacement for □. If the domain of □ is the set of counting numbers, then □ = 5 is the smallest. On the other hand, if rational numbers may be used as replacements, there is no replacement numeral which represents the smallest number of the truth set of this inequality.

The method of finding truth sets for equations in a systematic, rather than an intuitive manner is based on the relationships between operations.

If $a + b = c$, then $a = c - b$.
Therefore, if $x - 7 = 15$, then $x = 15 + 7$, or $x = 23$.

If $a \times b = c$, then $b = c \div a$.
Therefore, if $3x = 15$, then $x = 15 \div 3$ or $x = 5$.

If $\frac{a}{b} = c$, then $a = bc$.

Therefore, if $2y/3 = 8$, then $2y = 8 \times 3$, or $2y = 24$, and $y = 24 \div 2$, or $y = 12$.

Not only are equations the tool for understanding number relations, but they are also useful in a variety of applications of mathematics. In certain types of applications, the equation involves several variables, and is called a *formula*. Formulas are often abbreviations for computation instructions. For example, the formula for the area of the interior of a rectangle is $A = lw$. This formula says that the measure of the area of the rectangle equals the product of the measures of the length and width of the rectangle. The corresponding formula for the area of a circle is $A = \pi r^2$, where r is the radius of the circle.

Here are samples of other formulas:

Formula	Meaning of Variables
$d = 16t^2$	The number of feet (d) an object falls in t seconds when dropped from a cliff.
$h = 8 + \dfrac{18 - a}{2}$	The desirable number of hours (h) of sleep for a boy or girl whose age (a) $\not> 18$ (that is, is not greater than 18).
$W = \dfrac{300,000}{k}$	The wave length in meters (W) of a radio wave with a frequency of k kilocycles per second.
$P = 110 + \dfrac{a}{2}$	Desirable blood pressure (P) for a person whose age is (a).
$n = 10a$	The number of shingles (n) needed to cover a roof with an area of a square feet.
$s = \dfrac{c}{1 - p}$	The selling price (s) when the rate of profit on sales is p, and the cost to the seller is (c).
$c = \dfrac{n(n + 1)}{2}$	The number of possible connections (c) between (n) telephones.
$W = I^2 R$	The energy developed per second (W) when I amperes of current flow through a resistance of R ohms.
$B = \dfrac{l\,w\,h}{2.5}$	The number of bushels of corn (B) in a rectangular bin, l feet long, w feet wide, and h feet high.

Equations are also a useful tool in solving problems. The relationships expressed in the problem are translated into equations. The truth set for the equation becomes the answer for the question of the problem. Here is a simple example:

A purse contains nickels and dimes. The total amount of money is 50 cents, and there are 8 coins. How many nickels and dimes are there in the purse?

Let n represent the number of nickels and d the number of dimes. Then the value of the nickels is $5n$ and the dimes $10d$. The equations are:

1. $n + d = 8$
   or $n = 8 - d$ (This expresses the number of coins.)

2. $5n + 10d = 50$

   or, replacing n by $8 - d$, $5(8 - d) + 10d = 50$ (This expresses the value of the coins.)

   Hence, $40 - 5d + 10d = 50$,
   or $5d = 10$, and $d = 2$

   Then, $n = 8 - d$
   or $n = 8 - 2 = 6$

   There are 6 nickels and 2 dimes in the purse.

GRAPHING TRUTH SETS

A good way to illustrate the truth set of a mathematical sentence is by means of graphs. Simple equations and inequalities with one variable can be related to a graph on the number line.

If $x = 3$, then the graph of the truth set is one point:

If $x > 2$, then the graph is an infinite set of points:

Since 2 is not a member of the truth set, we use an open circle at $x = 2$.

If $x < 5$, then the graph of the truth set depends on the domain of x. If the replacement set for x is the counting numbers, then the truth set is $x = \{1, 2, 3, 4\}$, and the graph is a set of four points:

If the domain of x is the integers, the truth set of $x < 5$ is $x = \{4, 3, 2, 1, 0, ^-1, ^-2, \ldots\}$. The graph of this truth set is:

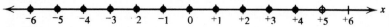

The arrow at the left indicates that the truth set extends without end to the left, including all negative integers.

If the domain of x is the positive rational numbers, the graph is:

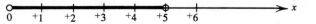

Since zero is not a positive rational number, it is not a member of the truth set.

If the domain of x is the set of all rational numbers, the graph of the truth set is:

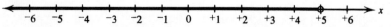

Graphs on the number line are also useful in illustrating the intersection or union of truth sets. Suppose that we want the truth sets for $x > {}^-3$ *and* $x < {}^+5$ in the domain of rational numbers. This is a compound condition. If x is to satisfy both conditions, we need the intersection of the truth sets for each equation. The truth set of $x > {}^-3$ includes rational numbers such as ${}^-2$, ${}^-\frac{1}{2}$, 0, ${}^+\frac{3}{4}$, ${}^+7$, and so on. The truth set of $x < {}^+5$ includes rational numbers such as ${}^+4$, ${}^+\frac{3}{4}$, 0, ${}^-2$, ${}^-6$, and so on. The graphs of the truth sets are as follows:

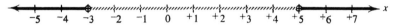

The intersection of the two truth sets is represented by the shaded line between ${}^-3$ and ${}^+5$. The truth set for $x > {}^-3$ *and* $x < {}^+5$ includes all rational numbers between ${}^-3$ and ${}^+5$.

In a similar way, open sentences with two variables can be represented by graphs. In this case a different number line is required for each variable. It is customary to use equal scales on each line and to consider the two number lines to be perpendicular, as drawn below:

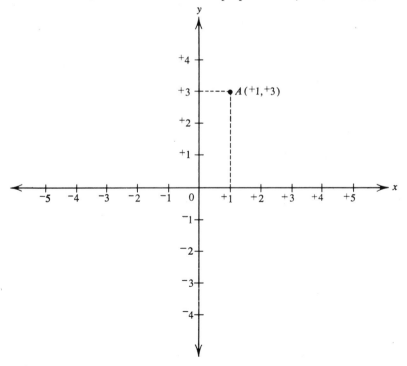

On this graph point A is located by the ordered pair (1, 3). For point A, $x = 1$ and $y = 3$. Then a set of ordered pairs with members such as (2, 4), (3, 5), (0, 2), (−2, 0) represents the operation of adding 2 to the first term of each ordered pair to get the second term. Another way to express this is by the equation $y = x + 2$. Then the graph of $y = x + 2$ is the set of points located by ordered pairs of the truth set as pictured below:

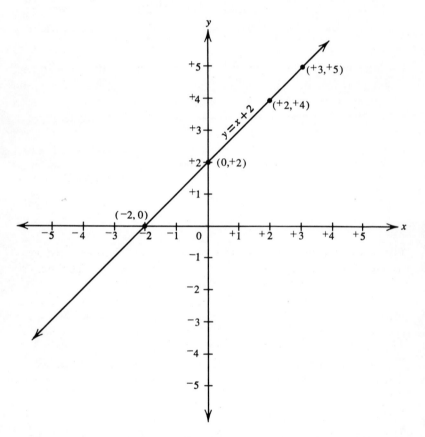

The graph above gives sums of 2 and any other number. At the elementary level graphs like this provide an interesting way to check calculations such as $5 + 2$, $^-1 + 2$, and $^-4 + 2$.

If we have an inequality in two variables such as $y > x + 2$, the graph of the truth set is the shaded region pictured on page 125.

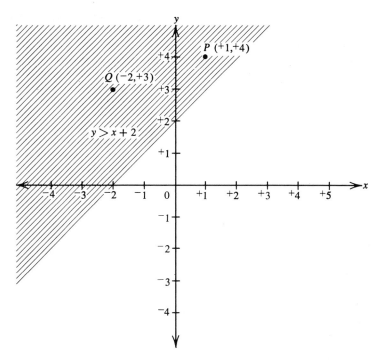

For this graph, ordered pairs such as (1, 4) and (−2, 3) are members of the truth set since $4 > 1 + 2$, and $3 > ^-2 + 2$. The points $P(1, 4)$ and $Q(^-2, 3)$ are points in the shaded region.

Equations and inequalities can be used to select a truth set. Hence, these sentences are sometimes called *set selectors*, or *set builders*. For example, the equation $y = x + 2$ selects replacements for x and y which make the sentence true. This truth set may be described as "the set of all ordered pairs (x, y) such that $y = x + 2$." The notation that is used for this statement is:

$$\{(x, y) : y = x + 2\}$$

The symbol ":" is used for the expression "such that." Then $\{x : x + 5 = 9\}$ is translated "the set of all x such that $x + 5 = 9$."

USING EQUATIONS AND INEQUALITIES IN PROBABILITY

Probability, risk, and chance are a part of our life from birth to death. Accidents, storms, fires, earthquakes are usually related to our lives by chance. The friends we make, the products we buy, the insects we see are usually the result of chance encounters. The cosmic rays from space, the raindrops from a storm, the molecules we breathe are usually arranged in a random way so that those we contact are due to chance. Since probability is such a common experience, it would seem appropriate for it to be included in school mathematics.

Even though most events occur by chance we can often predict future events. We can predict that about half the children that will be born in a given year will be boys. We predict that about 40,000 persons will be killed by automobile accidents next year. We can predict that tossed coins will usually turn up heads half of the time. But we cannot predict that a *certain* person will be killed in an accident. And we can't predict that a *certain* coin will turn up heads when it is tossed at random.

One way to get an estimate of how often an event happens is to perform experiments. These experiments give us samples of events. One of the easiest experiments for prediction is to toss a coin.

If the coin is well balanced, we say it is *just as likely* to turn up heads as tails. And we think of our tosses as being *random* tosses. Even so you can be quite sure that you will not get 50 heads in 50 sample tosses. Mathematicians have figured out that this would happen only about once in 1,000,000,000,000,000 tosses (or about once in a million billion tosses). Most of the results in experiments of 50 tosses will have more than 18 heads and less than 32 heads.

The probabilities of other events can also be checked by experiments. These experiments may involve spinning a dial, tossing dice, drawing cards from a deck, or selecting marbles from a sock. In each experiment we can check the results with the expected results. Current data such as weather reports, athletic records, school surveys, mortality tables, or stock market reports provide information for estimating the probabilities of daily events.

We express a probability as a fraction. If the probability of a certain event taking place is 1 out of 6, we write the probability as $\frac{1}{6}$. If an event is certain to happen, we say the probability is 1. Thus, the probability that a ball tossed up into the air will return to earth is 1. When an event is impossible or completely unlikely to occur, we say the probability is 0. Thus, the probability that you can live under water without mechanical aids for five hours is 0.

Another way to study probability is to use the graphs and truth sets of equations and inequalities. Suppose that we have 2 dice—one red (R), the other green (G). When these dice are tossed, they can turn up in 36 different ways, as follows:

$$(1, 1) \ (1, 2) \ (1, 3) \ (1, 4) \ (1, 5) \ (1, 6)$$
$$(2, 1) \ (2, 2) \ (2, 3) \ (2, 4) \ (2, 5) \ (2, 6)$$
$$(3, 1) \ (3, 2) \ (3, 3) \ (3, 4) \ (3, 5) \ (3, 6)$$
$$(4, 1) \ (4, 2) \ (4, 3) \ (4, 4) \ (4, 5) \ (4, 6)$$
$$(5, 1) \ (5, 2) \ (5, 3) \ (5, 4) \ (5, 5) \ (5, 6)$$
$$(6, 1) \ (6, 2) \ (6, 3) \ (6, 4) \ (6, 5) \ (6, 6)$$

The set of ordered pairs representing the events for dice tossing is called a *cartesian* product. The cartesian product of $R \times G$ is the set of all the 36 ordered pairs which represent different ways a red and green die can turn up. $R \times G = \{(1, 1) \ (1, 2) \ldots (6, 5) \ (6, 6)\}$, where $R = \{1, 2, 3, 4, 5, 6\}$ and $G = \{1, 2, 3, 4, 5, 6\}$.

One way to picture these possible tosses is to draw a lattice of points, as follows:

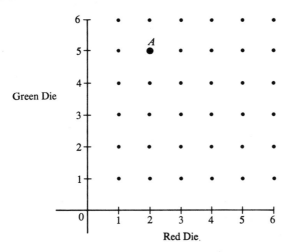

Then the toss $(2, 5)$ corresponds to point A. Similarly, each point of our lattice can be located by an ordered pair. Each ordered pair and each point represent one way the tossed dice can turn up.

Suppose we try to find all ordered pairs whose sum is 7. In set-builder notation, we would write $\{(R, G) : R + G = 7\}$. We find that there are 6 such ordered pairs: $(1, 6) \ (2, 5) \ (3, 4) \ (4, 3) \ (5, 2) \ (6, 1)$. On our lattice this is pictured as follows:

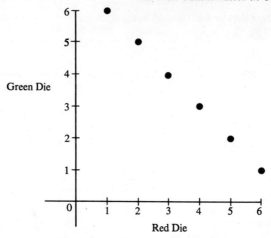

Strangely enough, these points seem to lie on a straight line. How many points are there in the truth set for $R + G = 7$? How many different ways in all can two dice fall? From these results we say that 6 out of 36 possible different tosses of two dice give a total of 7 dots. Thus, the chances or probability of tossing 7 dots with two dice is 6 in 36 or $\frac{1}{6}$.

Next consider an inequality on this lattice. What tosses result in the green die turning up a 5 or 6 dots? The inequality is $G > 4$. The points of our lattice for the truth set of this inequality are pictured like this:

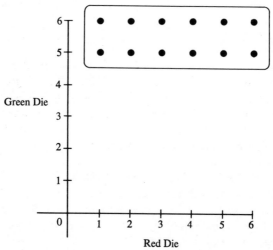

Now consider the compound statement:

$$\{(R, G): R + G = 7 \text{ and } G > 4\}$$

The graph below shows that this intersection is two events: namely, $(1, 6)$ and $(2, 5)$. Does it seem reasonable that the probability of these events is $\frac{2}{36}$?

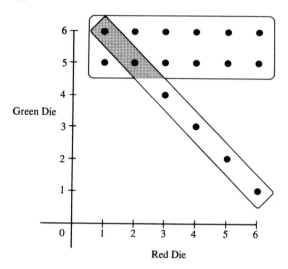

For the union of these two events, we want the set:

$$\{(R, G): R + G = 7 \text{ or } G > 4\}$$

or $\qquad \{(R, G): R + G = 7\} \cup \{(R, G): G > 4\}$

There are 16 points in this union. It appears that the probability of tossing a total of 7 dots *or* more than 4 dots on the green die is $\frac{16}{36}$.

This lattice above is sometimes called a *sample space*. A sample space is a set of points in which each point represents an event. There are 36 sample points in the sample space representing the different ways two dice can fall when tossed together.

FINDING TRUTH SETS OF EQUATIONS AND INEQUALITIES

Finding the truth sets for open sentences is still one of the major concerns of algebra. But formerly an equation such as $x + 5 = 17$ was solved by "transformation." You "move" the 5 to the right side and change the "sign," thus $x = 17 - 5$. This has been likened to a boy jumping a fence and landing upside down. The modern approach to solving equations is to base the solution on a few basic properties of operations and of equality. Then solving equations reinforces previous learning. Solving equations is not a bag of tricks; the steps can be defended by accepted definitions or assumptions.

Equality properties are now used to find the solution sets for equations. These properties are substitutions for statements such as "if equals are added to equals the results are equal."

1. Addition property of equality:
   Description: If $a = b$ and $c = d$, then $a + c = b + d$.
   Example: If $x - 3 = 7$ and $3 = 3$, then $x - 3 + 3 = 7 + 3$, or $x = 10$.

2. Multiplication property of equality:
   Description: If $a = b$ and $c = d$, then $ac = bc$.
   Example: If $\frac{1}{2}x = 7$ and $2 = 2$, then $(\frac{1}{2}x) \cdot 2 = 7 \cdot 2$, or $x = 14$.

3. Subtraction property of equality:
   Description: If $a = b$ and $c = d$, then $a - c = b - d$.
   Example: If $x + 8 = 19$ and $8 = 8$ then $x + 8 - 8 = 19 - 8$, or $x = 11$.

4. Division property of equality:
   Description: If $a = b$ and $c = d$ and $c \neq 0$ and $d \neq 0$, then
   $$\frac{a}{c} = \frac{b}{d}.$$
   Example: If $6x = 24$ and $6 = 6$ then $\frac{6x}{6} = \frac{24}{6}$, or $x = 4$.

5. Substitution property of equality:
   Description: If $a = b$ and $a = c$, then $c = b$.
   Example: If $x = 2y$ and $y = 9$, then $x = 2(9)$, or $x = 18$.

6. Reflexive property of equality:
   Description: If a is a number, then $a = a$.
   Example: If 3 is a number, then $3 = 3$.

7. Symmetric property of equality:
   Description: If $a = b$, then $b = a$.
   Example: If $5 = x$, then $x = 5$.

8. Transitive property of equality:
   Description: If $a = b$ and $b = c$, then $a = c$.
   Example: If $x = y$ and $y = 7$ then $x = 7$.

Here is an example of how the equality properties are used to solve equations (open sentences) in a logical fashion.

Find the solution set for $95 = 3x + 8$.

Statements	*Reasons*
1. $95 = 3x + 8$	1. Given
2. $95 - 8 = 3x + 8 - 8$	2. Subtraction property of equality
3. $87 = 3x$	3. Substitution property of equality
4. $87 \div 3 = 3x \div 3$	4. Division property of equality
5. $29 = x$	5. Substitution property of equality
6. $x = 29$	6. Symmetric property of equality

Similarly, inequality properties are used to find the solution sets for inequalities. Note that negative numbers sometimes produce unexpected results when used as multipliers or divisors.

1. Addition properties of inequalities:
   Description: If $a > b$ and $c = d$, then $a + c > b + d$.
   Example: If $x - 3 > 5$ and $3 = 3$, then $x - 3 + 3 > 5 + 3$, or $x > 8$.
   Description: If $a > b$ and $c > d$, then $a + c > b + d$.
   Example: If $8 > 5$ and $3 > 2$, then $8 + 3 > 5 + 2$, or $11 > 7$.

2. Multiplication properties of inequalities:
   Description: If $a > b$ and $c > 0$, then $ac > bc$.
   Example: If $\frac{x}{3} > 5$ and $3 > 0$, then $\left(\frac{x}{3}\right) \cdot 3 > 5 \cdot 3$, or $x > 15$.
   Description: If $a > b$ and $c < 0$, then $ac < bc$.
   Example: If $6 > {}^-4$ and ${}^-2 < 0$, then $6 \cdot (^-2) < (^-4)(^-2)$, or ${}^-12 < 8$.

3. Division properties of inequalities:
   Description: If $a > b$ and $c > 0$, then $\frac{a}{c} > \frac{b}{c}$.
   Example: If $3x > 15$ and $3 > 0$, then $\frac{3x}{3} > \frac{15}{3}$, or $x > 5$.
   Description: If $a > b$ and $c < 0$, then $\frac{a}{c} < \frac{b}{c}$.
   Example: If $12 > {}^-6$ and ${}^-3 < 0$, then $\frac{12}{^-3} < \frac{^-6}{^-3}$, or ${}^-4 < 2$.

4. Substitution property of inequalities:
   Description: If $a > b$ and $a = c$, then $c > b$.
   Example: If $x > y$ and $y = 10$, then $x > 10$.

5. Reflexive property of inequalities:
    Description: If a and b are any 2 different real numbers then
    $$a < b \text{ or } b > a \text{ but not both.}$$
    Example: If $x < 5$, then $x \not> 5$.

6. Symmetric property of inequalities:
    Description: If $a > b$, then $b < a$.
    Example: If $x > 8$, then $8 < x$.

7. Transitive property of inequalities:
    Description: If $a > b$ and $b > d$ then $a > d$.
    Example: If $x > y$ and $y > 12$, then $x > 12$.

LINEAR PROGRAMMING

Graphs of inequalities are often used in industry to plan its work and make other important decisions by a method called *linear programming*. Here is a simple example to illustrate this method.

A certain company makes skis and golf clubs.   Two different machines, A and B, are used to make these articles.   To produce one pair of skis requires 3 hours on machine A and 2 hours on B.   To make a golf club requires 1 hour on machine A and 2 hours on B.

The company makes a profit of \$10.00 on each pair of skis and \$4.00 on each golf club.   How should machines A and B be scheduled in order to make the greatest profit?   To answer this question a graph of several inequalities is used.

Let x represent the number of skis and y the number of golf clubs produced in one day.   Assume that each machine may run 12 hours per day or less.   On machine A, x skis use $3x$ hours of time and y clubs require $1y$ hours.   The inequality for the total daily time on machine A is:

$$3x + y \leq 12$$

(Where "$\leq$" is read "less than or equal to.")

For machine B the time inequality is

$$2x + 2y \leq 21$$

Since the number of skis or clubs produced per day cannot be less than zero we have these inequalities:

$$x \geq 0, \qquad y \geq 0$$

The graphs of these inequalities are as follows:

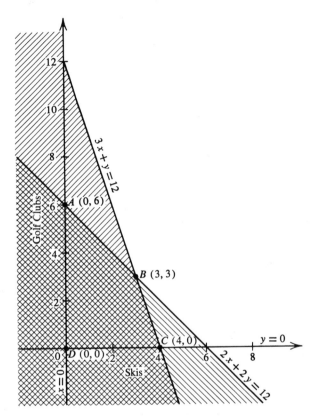

Note that *A*, *B*, *C*, and *D* are the vertices (corners) of a polygon (many-sided figure). The interior of this polygon is the intersection of the truth sets of all four inequalities. The coordinates of these vertex points represent the following values for x and y:

$$A \ (x = 0, y = 6) \qquad B \ (x = 3, y = 3)$$
$$C \ (x = 4, y = 0) \qquad D \ (x = 0, y = 0)$$

Since the profit is \$10.00 per pair of skis and \$4.00 per club, the total profit (*P*) for x pairs of skis and y clubs is

$$P = 10x + 4y$$

It happens that the maximum profit will be obtained at one of the vertices of the polygon graph. Which of these points represents the greatest profit?

At A ($x = 0$, $y = 6$): $P = 10x + 4y = 10(0) + 4(6) = 24$
At B ($x = 3$, $y = 3$): $P = 10x + 4y = 10(3) + 4(3) = 42$
At C ($x = 4$, $y = 0$): $P = 10x + 4y = 10(4) + 4(0) = 40$
At D ($x = 0$, $y = 0$): $P = 10x + 4y = 10(0) + 4(0) = 0$

From the above profit equalities it is evident that the maximum profit ($42.00) is obtained at point B, where $x = 3$ and $y = 3$. Thus, the greatest profit for a 12-hour day for machines A and B is to schedule 3 pair of skis and 3 golf clubs.

EXERCISES

1. Indicate whether or not the following sentences are true (T), false (F), or open (O).
   a. $78 + 91 = 91 + 78$
   b. $35 + \square = \square$
   c. $\square + 17 = 68$
   d. $3x + 18 = 30$
   e. $3(x + y) = 3x + 3y$
2. Translate the following statements into equations or inequalities.
   a. The product of a number multiplied by 5 is 20.
   b. The sum of a number and 16 is 42.
   c. The difference between 17 and my age is 3.
   d. If a certain number is doubled, then it is 5 more than 17.
   e. The value of n eight-cent stamps is 96 cents.
3. Find the truth set for each of the following open sentences.
   a. $x + 7 = 19$
   b. $y - 4 = 31$
   c. $3 \times \square = 14 + \square$
   d. $5w + 8 = 53$
   e. $\triangle(\triangle + 3) = 4$
4. Find three members of the truth set for each of these set selectors if the domain of x and y is the counting numbers.
   a. $\{x : x > {}^-2\}$
   b. $\{\square : \square < 7\}$
   c. $\{x : x + 3 > 3\}$
   d. $\{y : y - 6 < 10\}$
   e. $\{(x, y) : x + y = 10\}$

5. Give the justification for each step in finding the truth set for $5x + 7 = 82$.
   a. If $5x + 7 = 82$, then $5x + 7 = 75 + 7$.
   b. If $5x + 7 = 75 + 7$, then $5x = 75$.
   c. If $5x = 75$, then $x = 75 \div 5$.
   d. If $x = 75 \div 5$, then $x = 15$.

6. Sketch the graphs of the truth sets for these equations. Assume the domain of x and y is the rational numbers.
   a. $x = 7$
   b. $x > {}^{-}5$
   c. $x < 6$
   d. $y = 2x$
   e. $y < x + 5$

PATTERNS IN MATHEMATICS

9

Mathematics has been described, at least in part, as the study of patterns, where by a pattern we mean any kind of regularity of form or idea. Investigating an array of data for some kind of pattern can be one of the most stimulating and creative activities in mathematics. In studying patterns for the secrets they can yield, today's mathematics students are in a real sense engaging in the kind of activity that has led to some of the most profound discoveries in mathematics. The study of patterns puts a student on his mettle, for not only must he bring to bear a knowledge of the subject, but he must also give free rein to the imaginative, speculative side of his nature. Traditional mathematics, traditionally taught, seldom allowed students, even the gifted ones, to strengthen their imaginative ability in mathematics. The best of the newer programs encourage even average students to look hard at sequences of numbers or geometric shapes and let their minds run over them to see if they can find what rules or relationships operate.

In this chapter, we shall present many different kinds of patterns, drawn largely from work with numbers. To start, perhaps somewhat unfairly, try to find the relationship among the following numbers and predict the number that should follow the last one shown here:

$$23 \quad 28 \quad 34 \quad 42 \quad 50 \quad 59 \quad 66 \quad 72$$

New Yorkers will probably be the only ones to recognize these numbers as stops on the Seventh Avenue subway and will know that 79 is the number that follows 72. If there is, then, no other pattern to this array of numbers, one should blame the planners of the line for not having been more systematic mathematically. We assure the reader that henceforth the other patterns studied in this chapter will be authentic ones.

Here, for example, is a famous sequence of numbers, first studied by the Italian mathematician Fibonacci about 1200 A.D. Can you find the pattern? Can you predict the next number?

$$1\ 1\ 2\ 3\ 5\ 8\ 13\ 21\ 34\ 55$$

The next number is, of course, 89, because each number is formed by adding the two previous numbers—$1 + 1 = 2$; $1 + 2 = 3$, and so forth.

NUMBERS AND SHAPES

One way to study the pattern of numbers is to represent them with dots. Then some numbers are seen to be *triangular numbers*.

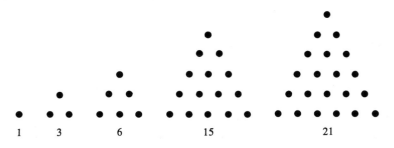

What is the next triangular number? Triangular numbers are related to sums:

$$1 = 1$$
$$1 + 2 = 3$$
$$1 + 2 + 3 = 6$$
$$1 + 2 + 3 + 4 = 10$$
$$1 + 2 + 3 + 4 + 5 = 15$$
$$1 + 2 + 3 + 4 + 5 + 6 = 21$$

Hence the next triangular number is $1 + 2 + 3 + 4 + 5 + 6 + 7$. What is this sum?

How many triangular numbers are there? Since there is no end to the number of counting numbers these additions may be continued without end.

Some counting numbers are *square numbers*.

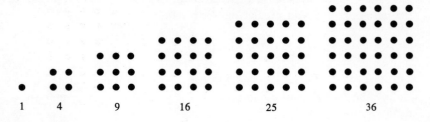

| 1 | 4 | 9 | 16 | 25 | 36 |

What is the next square number? We can find the square numbers by multiplication.

$$1 \times 1 = 1 \quad 2 \times 2 = 4 \quad 3 \times 3 = 9 \quad 4 \times 4 = 16$$
$$5 \times 5 = 25 \quad 6 \times 6 = 36$$

We can also find square numbers by adding odd numbers.

$$1 + 3 = 4$$
$$1 + 3 + 5 = 9$$
$$1 + 3 + 5 + 7 = 16$$
$$1 + 3 + 5 + 7 + 9 = 25$$
$$1 + 3 + 5 + 7 + 9 + 11 = 36$$

Then the next square number is $1 + 3 + 5 + 7 + 9 + 11 + 13$. What is this sum?

Why is there no end to the number of square numbers?

Since square numbers are the sums of odd numbers they are also formed by adding triangular numbers.

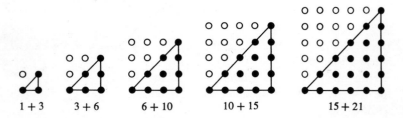

| 1 + 3 | 3 + 6 | 6 + 10 | 10 + 15 | 15 + 21 |

If we use the even numbers we obtain *rectangular numbers*.

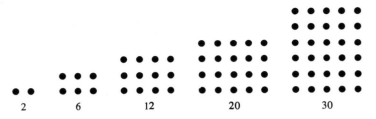

| 2 | 6 | 12 | 20 | 30 |

What is the next rectangular number? We can find rectangular numbers by the addition of even numbers.

$$2 = 2$$
$$2 + 4 = 6$$
$$2 + 4 + 6 = 12$$
$$2 + 4 + 6 + 8 = 20$$
$$2 + 4 + 6 + 8 + 10 = 30$$

Thus the next rectangular number is $2 + 4 + 6 + 8 + 10 + 12$. What is this sum? Why is there no end to the number of rectangular numbers?

Another way to find the rectangular numbers is by multiplication.

$$1 \times 2 = 2 \quad 2 \times 3 = 6 \quad 3 \times 4 = 12 \quad 4 \times 5 = 20$$
$$5 \times 6 = 30$$

Another set of numbers is called *pentagonal numbers*.

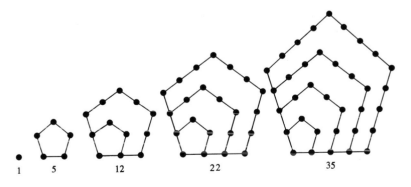

| 1 | 5 | 12 | 22 | 35 |

What is the next pentagonal number? Pentagonal numbers are obtained by adding triangular numbers and square numbers.

Triangular numbers		Square numbers		Pentagonal numbers
0	+	1	=	1
1	+	4	=	5
3	+	9	=	12
6	+	16	=	22
10	+	25	=	25
15	+	36	=	?

The dot pattern for these sums looks like this:

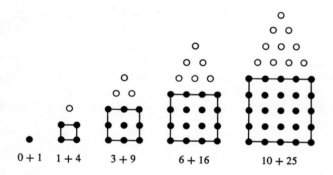

0 + 1   1 + 4   3 + 9   6 + 16   10 + 25

Another famous number triangle is Pascal's triangle.

1
1 1
1 2 1
1 3 3 1
1 4 6 4 1
1 5 10 10 5 1
1 6 15 20 15 6 1
1 7 21 35 35 21 7 1

1. What is the pattern of the sum of each row?

   1,   1 + 1,   1 + 2 + 1,   1 + 3 + 3 + 1,   1 + 4 + 6 + 4 + 1,
   1 + 5 + 10 + 10 + 5 + 1,   1 + 6 + 15 + 20 + 15 + 6 + 1,
   1 + 7 + 21 + 35 + 35 + 21 + 7 + 1

2. What do you predict the sum of the next row to be?
3. What do you predict to be the number below 21 in the next row? You can find it by writing the next term for the chain 1, 3, 6, 10, 15, 21, __.
4. How is the term in one row related to the sum of two terms above it?
5. What do you predict to be all the numbers in the next row?
6. How are the numbers of the following triangle related to Pascal's triangle?

$$11\ ?$$
$$11 \times 11?$$
$$11 \times 11 \times 11?$$
$$11 \times 11 \times 11 \times 11?$$

It happens that Pascal's triangle is very useful in the study of probability.

PRIME NUMBER PATTERNS?

The search for patterns has perhaps been no more diligent than in the branch of mathematics known as the theory of numbers, especially in that section that involves the study of prime numbers. A prime number, you will recall, is a number that cannot be divided evenly by any number except itself and 1. Thus 37 is a prime number because it can be divided evenly only by 37 and 1. Mathematicians for hundreds of years have been trying to find some regularity to the way in which prime numbers are distributed. The ancient Greek mathematician Eratosthenes devised a simple scheme for finding prime numbers less than 100. In the so-called "Sieve of Eratosthenes," the first 100 numbers are set out in an array and all but the prime numbers are eliminated. This is done by eliminating first the multiples of 2, then the multiples of 3, and so forth. The sieve then presents this appearance:

X ② ③ X ⑤ X ⑦ X X

X ⑪ X ⑬ X X X ⑰ X ⑲

X X X ㉓ X X X X X ㉙

X ㉛ X X X X X ㊲ X X

X ㊸ X ㊹ X X X ㊼ X X

X X X ㊾ X X X X X ㊾

X ㊿ X X X X X ㊻ X X

X ㊼ X ⑦③ X X X X X ㊼

X X X ㊼③ X X X X X ㊼⑨

X X X X X X X ㊼⑦ X X

Is there a pattern here? If there is, no one has yet been able to discover it. But the search goes on.

PATTERNS WITH COUNTING NUMBERS

Here is a famous number pattern for counting numbers:

COUNTING NUMBER TABLE

0	1	2	3	4	5	6	7	8	9
10	11	12	13	14	15	16	17	18	19
20	21	22	23	24	25	26	27	28	29
30	31	32	33	34	35	36	37	38	39
40	41	42	43	44	45	46	47	48	49
50	51	52	53	54	55	56	57	58	59
60	61	62	63	64	65	66	67	68	69
70	71	72	73	74	75	76	77	78	79
80	81	82	83	84	85	86	87	88	89
90	91	92	93	94	95	96	97	98	99

1. What is the pattern of all even numbers?
2. What is the pattern of all numbers that are multiples of 3? 4? 5?
3. Cross out all numbers exactly divisible by 6. Are these numbers all even? Are they all multiples of 3?

4. Encircle all numbers exactly divisible by 8. Are these numbers all multiples of 4?
5. What is unusual about the pattern of numerals for numbers that are exactly divisible by 9?
6. What is the pattern of numerals for numbers that are exactly divisible by 8?

MAGIC SQUARES

A square pattern of numbers like the one below is called a *magic square*. Such squares have been curiosities for mathematicians for hundreds of years.

8	1	6
3	5	7
4	9	2

The sum of the numbers of each row and each column and each diagonal is 15. Whenever the sums of the rows, columns, and diagonals of a square number pattern are equal, we have a magic square. Hence, we can complete a magic square even when many numbers are missing.

What is the sum of the first column of the magic square below?

10	3	8
a	7	b
c	d	e

We start with the first row.

$$10 + 3 + 8 = 21$$

Then $3 + 7 + d = 21$,   or $d = 11$

Next $10 + 7 + e = 21$,   or $17 + e = 21$, and $e = 4$

$8 + 7 + c = 21$,   or $15 + c = 21$, and $c = 6$

For the first column

$$10 + a + c = 21$$

But $c = 6$, so $10 + a + 6 = 21$, and $a = 5$.
For the middle row

$$a + 7 + b = 21$$

But $a = 5$, so $5 + 7 + b = 21$, or $12 + b = 21$, and $b = 9$.

The patterns in magic squares, as we can see, can provide an intriguing way to practice addition. They can be extended to many more rows and columns.

PATTERNS IN ALGEBRA

The new mathematics programs also use number patterns to discover many relationships in algebra.

Notice the pattern of these two sets of operations using the number line.

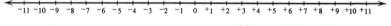

Subtraction on the number line	*Addition of the additive inverse of the minuend*
$^{+}8 - {}^{+}3 = {}^{+}5$	$^{+}8 + {}^{-}3 = {}^{+}5$
$^{+}8 - {}^{-}3 = {}^{+}11$	$^{+}8 + {}^{+}3 = {}^{+}11$
$^{-}8 - {}^{-}3 = {}^{-}5$	$^{-}8 + {}^{+}3 = {}^{-}5$
$^{-}8 - {}^{+}3 = {}^{-}11$	$^{-}8 + {}^{-}3 = {}^{-}11$
$^{+}3 - {}^{+}8 = {}^{-}5$	$^{+}3 + {}^{-}8 = {}^{-}5$
$^{+}3 - {}^{-}8 = {}^{+}11$	$^{+}3 + {}^{+}8 = {}^{+}11$
$^{-}3 - {}^{-}8 = {}^{+}5$	$^{-}3 + {}^{+}8 = {}^{+}5$

How do the answers to each subtraction example compare with the answers to the corresponding addition example? How do the first terms of the subtraction compare with the first terms of the addition? How do the second terms compare?

If you performed the subtractions and additions correctly, you obtained the same result for each pair. In other words, $^{+}8 - {}^{+}3 = {}^{+}8 + {}^{-}3$.

These results then suggest that we perform subtractions with directed numbers by addition. Instead of subtracting a number, we add its opposite or its *additive inverse*.

The abstract symbolism of algebra does not usually lend itself to visual patterns. However, there are exceptions, such as the following:

The equality $(a + b)^2 = (a + b)(a + b)$ can be represented by a square where a is the measure of one line and b is the measure of a second line.

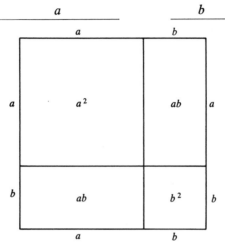

Then the area of the large square is $a^2 + ab + ab + b^2$ or $a^2 + 2ab + b^2$. Hence $(a + b)^2 = a^2 + 2ab + b^2$.

PATTERNS IN GEOMETRY

To show how a pattern of data is used to explore geometric ideas consider the following problem:

What is the maximum number of regions obtained when you make cuts all the way across a circular cake, without cutting through the same point more than twice.

The results give us the pattern on page 146.

If the pattern of this result continues we would predict 22 pieces from 6 cuts, 29 pieces from 7 cuts, and so on. The number chain for the number of pieces is 1, 2, 4, 7, 11, 16, 22, 29, 37, 46, ...

However, results based on number patterns can be misleading if based on too few cases or on special cases. Consider these calculations:

Multiplication	*Addition*
$2 \times 2 = 4$	$2 + 2 = 4$
$\frac{3}{2} \times 3 = 4\frac{1}{2}$	$\frac{3}{2} + 3 = 4\frac{1}{2}$
$\frac{4}{3} \times 4 = 5\frac{1}{3}$	$\frac{4}{3} + 4 = 5\frac{1}{3}$
$\frac{5}{4} \times 5 = 6\frac{1}{4}$	$\frac{5}{4} + 5 = 6\frac{1}{4}$

From this pattern we might conclude that we get the same result when adding or multiplying the same two numbers. But we know this is false. One counter example such as $3 + 3 = 6$ and $3 \times 3 = 9$ is sufficient to reject the conclusion. Thus, it is important to establish a conclusion on adequate evidence or on a logical proof.

Number of Cuts	Drawing	Number of Pieces	Increase in the Number of Pieces
0		1	0
1		2	1
2		4	2
3		7	3
4		11	4
5		16	5

PATTERNS WITH NINES

The multiples of 9 have a surprising pattern:

$$9 \times 2 = 18 \qquad\qquad 1 + 8 = 9$$
$$9 \times 3 = 27 \qquad\qquad 2 + 7 = 9$$
$$9 \times 7 = 63 \qquad\qquad 6 + 3 = 9$$
$$9 \times 25 = 225 \qquad\quad 2 + 2 + 5 = 9$$
$$9 \times 86 = 774 \qquad\quad 7 + 7 + 4 = 18,\; 1 + 8 = 9$$

This suggests that the sum formed by the digits of a multiple of 9 is 9 or another multiple of 9.

Which of these numbers are multiples of 9?

$$
\begin{array}{ll}
85 & 8 + 5 = 13 \\
486 & 4 + 8 + 6 = 18 \\
793 & 7 + 9 + 3 = 19 \\
3501 & 3 + 5 + 0 + 1 = 9
\end{array}
$$

The sum formed by the digits of the numeral for any number is also related to remainders when we divide by 9:

Number	Sum formed by digits	Division by
24	$2 + 4 = 6$	$24 \div 9 = 2 \, R \, 6$
47	$4 + 7 = 11, \ 1 + 1 = 2$	$47 \div 9 = 5 \, R \, 2$
346	$3 + 4 + 6 = 13, \ 1 + 3 = 4$	$346 \div 9 = 38 \, R \, 4$

These examples suggest this result: The sum formed by the digits for any counting number equals the remainder when we divide that number by 9.

This relationship gives us a way to check computations. It is called *casting out nines*.

This is how it works for addition.

$$
\begin{array}{ll}
26 & 2 + 6 = 8 \\
\underline{41} & \underline{4 + 1 = 5} \\
67 & 6 + 7 = 13 = 8 + 5
\end{array}
$$

Notice how the sums formed by digits of the numbers of the addition problems and the answers are related.

Here is the reason for our result:

$$
\begin{array}{rl}
26 = & 2 \text{ nines and } 8 \\
\underline{41} = & \underline{4 \text{ nines and } 5} \\
67 & 6 \text{ nines and } 13
\end{array}
$$

this method to check another addition.

$$
\begin{array}{ll}
142 & 1 + 4 + 2 = 7 \\
71 & 7 + 1 = 8 \\
35 & 3 + 5 = 8 \\
\hline
248 & 2 + 4 + 8 = 14 \\
& 1 + 4 = \boxed{5}
\end{array}
\qquad
\begin{array}{l}
7 + 8 + 8 = 23 \\
2 + 3 = \boxed{5}
\end{array}
$$

Notice that when our checking sums are greater than 9 we form new sums with the digits. Also, the sum formed by digits for our answer is the same as that for the sum of the original numbers. When we get the same results for the sums of digits in this way we usually have the correct answer. When the sums formed by digits do not agree we look for an error.

$$
\begin{array}{ll}
432 & 4 + 3 + 2 = 9 \\
28 & 2 + 8 = 10 \\
674 & 6 + 7 + 4 = 17 \qquad 9 + 10 + 17 = 36 \\
\hline
1124 & 1 + 1 + 2 + 4 = \boxed{8} \qquad\qquad 3 + 6 = \boxed{9}
\end{array}
$$

Since our results are different, 8 and 9, our sum, 1124, is probably wrong. What is the correct sum of $432 + 28 + 674$?

The casting out of nines can also be used to check multiplications.

$$
\begin{array}{cl}
& 123 \times 42 \\
123 & 1 + 2 + 3 = 6 \\
\times 42 & 4 + 2 = 6 \\
\hline
246 & 6 \times 6 = 36 \\
492 & 3 + 6 = \boxed{9} \\
\hline
5166 & 5 + 1 + 6 + 6 = 18, \; 1 + 8 = \boxed{9}
\end{array}
$$

Although this check may look difficult, it becomes easy with practice. Try another.

$$
\begin{array}{cl}
438 & 4 + 3 + 8 = 15 = 1 + 5 = 6 \\
\times 56 & 5 + 6 = 11 = 1 + 1 = 2 \\
\hline
2628 & 6 \times 2 = 12 = 1 + 2 = \boxed{3} \\
2180 & \\
\hline
24428 & 2 + 4 + 4 + 2 + 8 = 20 \qquad 2 + 0 = \boxed{2}
\end{array}
$$

Since our sums do not agree, there must be an error in our computation. What is the correct product for 438 × 56?

In a similar way we can check subtractions:

$$568 - 193$$

568	$5 + 6 + 8 = 19$
-193	$1 + 9 + 3 = 13$
375	$3 + 7 + 5 = 15$

$19 - 13 = \fbox{6}$

$1 + 5 = \fbox{6}$

EXERCISES

1. Find the sums of rows, columns, and diagonals to see if the patterns shown in a–f are magic squares.

a.

7	12	5
6	8	10
11	4	9

b.

10	9	14
15	11	7
8	13	12

c.

16	2	3	13
5	11	10	8
9	7	6	12
4	14	15	1

d.

1	12	7	14
8	13	2	11
10	3	16	5
15	6	9	4

e.

8	$4\frac{1}{2}$	7
$5\frac{1}{2}$	$6\frac{1}{2}$	$7\frac{1}{2}$
6	$8\frac{1}{2}$	5

f.

3.0	3.4	1.4
1.0	2.6	4.2
3.8	1.8	2.2

2. Find the missing numbers for the magic squares.

a.

10	11	6
5	9	13

b.

10	3	8
5	a	b
c	d	e

3. For each set of numbers below compare the numbers, find the pattern, then predict the missing numbers.

a. 3, 6, 9, 12, _____ _____ _____ .
b. 5, 10, 15, 20, _____ _____ _____ .
c. 1, 4, 7, 10, _____ _____ _____ .
d. 1, 2, 4, 8, _____ _____ _____ .
e. 4, 8, 12, 16, _____ _____ _____ .
f. 1, 6, 11, 16, _____ _____ _____ .
g. 2, 6, 10, 14, _____ _____ _____ .
h. 32, 16, 8, 4, _____ _____ _____ .
i. 1, 3, 9, 27, _____ _____ _____ .
j. 3, 6, 12, 24, _____ _____ _____ .
k. 1, 2, 4, 7, 11, _____ _____ _____ .
l. 10, 11, 9, 10, 8, _____ _____ _____ .
m. 1, 3, 4, 6, 7, 9, _____ _____ _____ .
n. 2, 5, 9, 14, 20, _____ _____ _____ .
o. 2, 7, 2, 9, 2, 11, _____ _____ _____ .
p. 0, 1, 4, 9, 16, _____ _____ _____ .

4. Study the number patterns in each problem. Then predict the missing parts of the pattern.

a. $1 \times 9 = 10 - 1$
   $2 \times 9 = 20 - 2$
   $3 \times 9 = 30 - 3$
   $4 \times 9 = \underline{\hspace{1cm}}$
   $\underline{\hspace{1cm}} = 50 - 5$

b. $1 \times 8 = 10 - 2$
   $2 \times 8 = 20 - 4$
   $3 \times 8 = 30 - 6$
   $\underline{\hspace{1cm}} = 40 - 8$
   $5 \times 8 = \underline{\hspace{1cm}}$

c. $10 - 1 = 9$
$100 - 1 = 99$
$1000 - 1 = 999$
$10,000 - 1 = \underline{\qquad}$
$\underline{\qquad} = 99999$

d. $10 = 10$
$10 \times 10 = 100$
$10 \times 10 \times 10 = 1000$
$10 \times 10 \times 10 \times 10 \times = \underline{\qquad}$
$\underline{\qquad\qquad\qquad} = 100,000$

e. $(1 \times 8) + 1 = 9$
$(12 \times 8) + 2 = 98$
$(123 \times 8) + 3 = 987$
$(1234 \times 8) + 4 = 987\underline{\quad}$
$(12345 \times \underline{\ }) + \underline{\ } = 98765$

f. $9 + 1 \quad = 10$
$90 + 10 \quad = 100$
$900 + 100 = 1000$
$9000 + 1000 = \underline{\qquad}$
$\underline{\qquad} = 100,000$

g. $(1 \times 9) - 1 = 08$
$(21 \times 9) - 1 = 188$
$(321 \times 9) - 1 = 2888$
$(4321 \times 9) - 1 = 3888\underline{\quad}$
$(54321 \times 9) - 1 = \underline{\ }88888$

h. $37 \times 3 = 111$
$37 \times 6 = 222$
$37 \times 9 = 333$
$37 \times 12 = \underline{\quad}$
$37 \times \underline{\quad} = 555$

i. $(0 \times 9) + 8 = 8$
$(9 \times 9) + 7 = 88$
$(98 \times 9) + 6 = 888$
$(987 \times 9) + 5 = \underline{\qquad}$
$(9876 \times 9) + \underline{\ } = 88888$

j. $1 \times 5 = \frac{1}{2} \times 10$
$2 \times 5 = \frac{2}{2} \times 10$
$3 \times 5 = \frac{3}{2} \times 10$
$4 \times 5 = \underline{\ } \times 10$
$\underline{\qquad} = \frac{5}{2} \times 10$

k. $1 \times 99 = 99$
$2 \times 99 = 198$
$3 \times 99 = 297$
$\underline{\ } \times 99 = 396$
$5 \times 99 = \underline{\qquad}$
$6 \times 99 = \underline{\qquad}$

l. $1 \times 999 = 999$
$2 \times 999 = 1998$
$3 \times 999 = 2997$
$\underline{\ } \times 999 = 3996$
$5 \times \underline{\qquad} = 499\underline{\ }$
$6 \times 999 = \underline{\qquad}$

5. Check these multiplications by casting out nines.
a. $43 \times 36 = 1548$
b. $78 \times 92 = 7166$
c. $5847 \times 763 = 4,461,261$

10

Of all the mathematics taught in the schools, geometry is the one mathematical subject that achieved maturity earliest. Long before the development of algebra and long before the invention of long division, the great Greek mathematician Euclid wrote a geometry text that contained the geometry which has been taught in our schools for hundreds of years. Euclidian geometry consisted of the definitions, axioms, and theorems of plane and solid geometry. The typical course in geometry consisted largely in memorizing these facts and proofs with little opportunity to exercise imagination or creative ability.

For some strange reason school geometry took little or no notice of significant developments in geometry after Euclid. For example, the French mathematician and philosopher, René Descartes (1596–1650) made a great contribution to mathematics with his development of *coordinate geometry*. Descartes' coordinate geometry effects a union between algebra and geometry and enables each subject to throw light on the other. Until recently coordinate geometry was not studied until college mathematics. Now many ideas of coordinate geometry are introduced in the new school mathematics.

Another significant development in geometry was the invention of non-Euclidian geometries. In the early 1800's mathematicians like Bolyai, Lobachevsky, and Riemann began to question some of Euclid's axioms. Up to this time, the axioms of Euclid had been regarded as self-evident truths which obviously corresponded to reality. The significance of the non-Euclidian geometries was that new mathematical structures could be built which did not depend on verification by experience or concrete representation.

Another important reconsideration of Euclid's geometry has influenced the new school geometry. Euclid stated certain definitions that have been found to be unsatisfactory. Such definitions as "A point is that which has no parts" and "A line is length without breadth" are easily recognized as being inadequate. As a result of the work of the German mathematician David Hilbert (1862–1943), some of the

Euclidian axioms were recast and some new ones which were thought to be needed were added.

At the same time that the foundation of geometry was being examined, other mathematical structures were being developed. As we have seen in an earlier chapter, the fundamental properties of our counting number system were brought to light by Giuseppe Peano. Other mathematical structures such as groups were also invented during the nineteenth century.

With this background we can now understand better the changes in geometry as it is presented in the new school mathematics. However, there is still considerable disagreement about the kind of new geometry content to be offered to students. Nevertheless, the new courses, as tentative as they may be, do have certain features in common which we will describe in a very brief digest.

GEOMETRY IN THE ELEMENTARY SCHOOL

In the new mathematics programs, geometry is not limited to the high school. Geometry is woven into all of the grades in elementary school mathematics. Of course, the subject is treated from an informal point of view. Usually, no proofs of statements about lines or figures are called for. The approach, rather, is intuitive; that is, if a statement about a geometric idea appears to be reasonable from a drawing or other representation, it is accepted and worked with as though it were true.

In the primary grades children are asked to draw lines to locate points and to form triangles and quadrilaterals. Circles are drawn and related to angles, triangles, and intersections. The classical constructions of equal angles, bisectors of angles, bisectors of segments, and perpendicular and parallel lines are included. These constructions are performed with straight edge and compasses, but also by paper folding.

The treatment of geometry in the intermediate grades becomes much more precise. Lines, angles, and polygons are defined as sets of points or unions or intersections of sets of points. The figures of geometry are related to the simple closed curves of topology. An introduction to the geometry of three dimensions is included with experience in representing solids by two-dimensional drawings.

The measurement of length and area has been given a broader foundation in the new courses. The approximate aspect of measurement is emphasized. The distinction between precision and accuracy of measurement is carefully made. Considerable work is given in computations with measures.

The list below suggests many geometric ideas that have been found to be appropriate for young children. When these geometric ideas are presented, the distinction is made between the picture of the term and the idea. Children are led to understand that the marks we make on paper to represent a point, line, circle, or cube are only pictures of these ideas.

1. *Lines.* The difference between pictures of straight lines, curved lines, jagged lines, and segments of straight lines are noted. Straight lines through one point and straight lines through two points are drawn.

2. *Relationships of Lines.* Pictures of lines that intersect are drawn. Comparison of the angles formed by intersecting lines, perpendicular lines, and parallel lines are made.

3. *Comparison of Lines.* Comparison of the lengths of straight lines is made by using the symbols $<$ for "less than" and $>$ for "greater than." Straight lines of equal length are identified as congruent lines. Children learn to bisect a line, divide a straight line into four equal parts, double a straight line. They form a line which has a length equal to the sum of two lines and a line which has a length equal to the difference of two lines.

4. *Geometric Figures.* Pupils connect points to form pictures of a triangle, rectangle, square, parallelogram, quadrilateral, pentagon, and hexagon. They identify different geometric figures and compare the lengths of sides, diagonals, and the sizes of the angles of geometric figures.

5. *Circles.* Children learn to draw circles, with diameters, radii, chords, and arcs. Then they use the circle to draw hexagons and other symmetric designs.

6. *Solids.* Pupils make models of cubes, prisms, pyramids, cones, cylinders, and tetrahedrons out of cardboard. They identify objects and compare the corners, edges, and faces of each solid.

GEOMETRY IN THE SECONDARY SCHOOL

The new geometry is similar to traditional geometry in many ways. It still places major emphasis on logic and proof. But the logical structure is changed considerably by introducing new definitions, new assumptions, and new ways of organizing proofs. And the content is changed by introducing many new topics.

The content of traditional tenth-grade geometry usually included these topics:

Points, lines, and angles.
Plane figures—triangles, quadrilaterals, polygons, and circles.
Constructions and the locus of points.
Measures of angles, perimeters, and area.
The right triangle and trigonometry.

The new geometry includes all the topics listed above with the possible exception that little time is given to loci and constructions. In addition to new treatment of these old topics the following new topics are introduced:

Coordinate geometry.
Solid geometry.
Vectors.
Other geometries—non-Euclidean, projective, finite.
Topology and transformations.

However the greatest change in geometry is its new emphasis on structure. New definitions are stated, new assumptions made, and new proofs are presented. As of now, few new applications have been given even in our age of exploration of space.

OLD TERMS WITH NEW MEANINGS

The new geometry begins with an undefined element called a *point*. Then a *line* is defined as a certain infinite set of points. This line is considered to be a continuous set of points, with no "gaps" or "holes" in the line. A line is said to be *dense;* that is, another point can always be found between two points no matter how close together they are. Similarly, a plane is considered to be continuous and infinite in extent. A point on a line separates the line into two *half-lines.* The union of this point and one of the half-lines is a *ray.* If two rays have a common end point then the union of the two rays is an *angle.* If there are two points on a line, the line is separated into two half-lines and a *segment.*

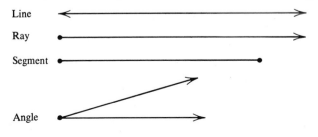

Line

Ray

Segment

Angle

A plane is also a set of points. And a triangle of a plane is the union of three segments. Thus a triangle is a set of points, a subset of the plane. Similarly, a polygon is a set of points, the union of a set of segments which separates the plane into two distinct regions, an interior region and an exterior region. Then the intersections of lines or the intersections of polygons are the intersections of sets of points. If the intersection set of two lines in the same plane is the empty set then the lines are parallel.

A circle is also a certain set of points of a plane. If the intersection set of a line of a given plane and a circle on the same plane is one point then the line is tangent to the circle.

Similarly, space is a set of points. A plane may be a set of lines and space may be a set of planes. Thus a line is a subset of a plane, and a plane is a subset of a space. The union of two half planes with a common boundary line is a dihedral angle.

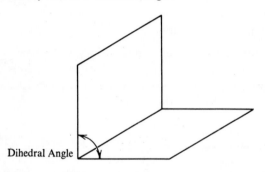

Dihedral Angle

The geometry of the plane is still concerned with congruence. But congruence is extended. The new geometry talks about congruent segments, congruent angles, and congruent circles, as well as congruent triangles. This congruence is also stated in new terms: "A one-to-one correspondence between the vertices of two triangles in which the corresponding parts are congruent is called a congruence between the two triangles."

The definition of similarity also illustrates new terminology: "Similar polygons are polygons which for some pairing of vertices, have corresponding angles equal and corresponding sides in proportion."

In presenting a congruence ($\cong$) or similarity of two triangles the notation is such that the correspondence is clear. If $\triangle ABC \cong \triangle DEF$, then $\angle A \cong \angle D$, $\angle B \cong \angle E$, $\overline{AB} \cong \overline{DE}$ and $\overline{AC} \cong \overline{DF}$, and so on. Hence A corresponds to D, B to E, and C to F.

The new geometry is made more precise by improving the symbolism. In the past AB might be used as the symbol for a line, a segment, or the measure of a segment. This ambiguity is no longer permissible. The following table indicates graphically how precise the new terms are.

NEW SYMBOLS FOR GEOMETRY

Name	Picture	New Symbol
Line	$A \quad B$	$\overleftrightarrow{AB}$
Segment	$A \quad B$	$\overline{AB}$
measure of segment $\overline{AB}$	- - - - - - - - - - - - - - - -	$m(\overline{AB})$
Ray	$A \quad B$	$\overrightarrow{AB}$
Angle	A $B \quad C$	$\angle ABC$
The measure of $\angle ABC$	A $B \quad C$	$m \angle ABC$
Definition of an angle	A $B \quad C$	$\overrightarrow{BA} \cup \overrightarrow{BC}$
Intersection of two lines	$C \quad B$ $A \quad E \quad D$	$\overleftrightarrow{AB} \cap \overleftrightarrow{CD} = \{E\}$
Definition of parallel lines	$A \quad B$ $C \quad D$	$\overleftrightarrow{AB} \cap \overleftrightarrow{CD} = \varnothing$

In order to make geometry a more complete mathematical structure old axioms, sometimes called *postulates*, are restated, and new postulates are added. Some of the new postulates are needed to relate geometric ideas to coordinates of number lines.

1. Every line contains at least two points.
2. Exactly one line lies on any two given points.

3. Every line in a plane separates the plane into two sets, called half-planes, each of which is convex.

4. Two congruent line segments are two line segments which have equal measures.

5. To every line segment, $\overline{AB}$, there corresponds exactly one positive real number, AB, the distance between the points A and B.

6. If B lies between A and C, then $AB + BC = AC$.

7. To every angle, ABC, there corresponds a real number between $0°$ and $180°$ called the measure of the angle.

8. Given a correspondence between two triangles. If two sides and the included angle of the first triangle are congruent to the corresponding parts of the second triangle, then the correspondence is a congruence.

Note the emphasis on sets, real numbers, and correspondence in these statements.

Every effort is made to make each topic in geometry a complete mathematical structure by itself. Of course, each topic is dependent on previous postulates and definitions. Area is a topic which is typical of the new treatment.

We begin by stating these definitions:

1. A polygonal region is the union of the polygon and its interior.
2. The area of a region is a unique positive number.
3. The area of a square with side one unit long is 1.
4. The area of a region is then the number of square units contained in the region.

We will also need some postulates:

1. If two polygons are congruent, then the areas of the polygonal regions are equal.
2. If the intersection of two polygonal regions does not include any interior points of the regions, then the area of the union of these regions is the sum of their areas.
3. The area of a rectangle is the product of the measures of two adjacent sides.

With these definitions and postulates it is possible to prove theorems about areas such as "the area of a triangle is half the product of the measure of the base and the measure of the altitude." As a result of these proofs, formulas are derived to express the area of parallelograms, trapezoids, regular polygons, circles, and irregular regions. Thus, the study of the area of a geometric figure illustrates a mathematical structure based on assumptions, definitions, and theorems.

COORDINATE GEOMETRY

One of the basic innovations of the new geometry, as we have pointed out, is to make coordinate geometry part of the structure of geometry. To do this requires some new postulates, such as the following:

1. To every point, there corresponds exactly one real number.
2. To every real number, there corresponds exactly one point.
3. The coordinate system may be shown so that any point on a line may serve as the origin.

Having established a coordinate system for number lines, it is appropriate to use these coordinates for definitions, descriptions, and proofs:

1. The graph of $x \geq 0$ is a ray.

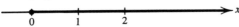

2. The graph of $x > y$ is a half-plane.

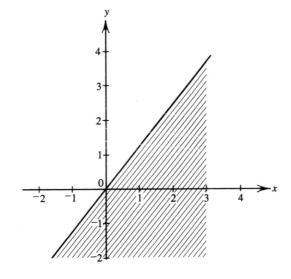

3. The set $\{(x, y):(x + y < 7) \text{ and } (x > 2) \text{ and } (y > 1)\}$ is the interior of a triangle.

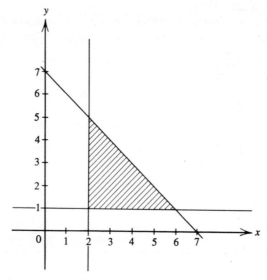

4. The graphs of $y = 7$ and $y = 3$ are parallel lines. Similarly, the graphs of $x + 2y = 9$ and $x + 2y = 17$ are parallel lines.
5. The graphs of $x = 4$ and $y = 3$ are perpendicular lines. Similarly, the graphs of $x + 2y = 9$ and $2x - y = 12$ are perpendicular lines.
6. The graph of $x^2 + y^2 = 25$ is a circle.
7. The graph of $x^2 + y^2 < 25$ is the interior of a circle.
8. The union of $\overline{AB}$, $\overline{BC}$, and $\overline{CD}$ with endpoints at $A(5, 0)$, $B(5, 9)$, and $C(12, 0)$ is a right triangle.
9. The points $A(3, 2)$, $B(5, 5)$, $C(11, 7)$, $D(9, 4)$ are the vertices of a parallelogram.

The distance postulate and the Pythagorean theorem are used to derive the formula for the distance (d) between two points on a plane. If A has coordinates (x_1, y_1) and B, coordinates (x_2, y_2), then

$$AB = \sqrt{(x_2 - x_1)^2 + (y_2 - y_1)^2}$$

This formula can be used to find the coordinates of the midpoints of lines or of points which divide a line in a given proportion. Next, the slopes of lines are determined. The slope of the graph of $y = 2x + 3$ is 2. Using slopes and coordinates of points it is possible to write the equation for the graphs of any straight line. If we can describe a line with an equation we now have a new tool for the analysis of geometric figures.

This information can be used to prove some theorems in a new way.

THEOREM: The diagonals of a rectangle are congruent.
GIVEN: Rectangle $ABCD$
PROVE: $\overline{AC} \cong \overline{BD}$

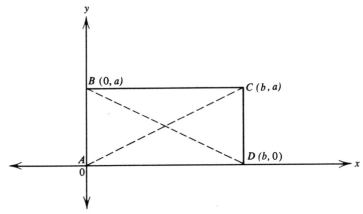

PROOF: Use a coordinate system so that the coordinates of the vertices are the following: $A(0, 0)$, $B(0, a)$, $C(b, a)$, $D(b, 0)$.

Length of $\overline{AC}$: $\overline{AC} = \sqrt{(b - 0)^2 + (a - 0)^2} = \sqrt{b^2 + a^2}$
Length of $\overline{BD}$: $\overline{BD} = \sqrt{(0 - b)^2 + (0 - a)^2} = \sqrt{b^2 + a^2}$
Therefore $\overline{AC} = \overline{BD}$, and $\overline{AC} \cong \overline{BD}$.

The proof in traditional geometry used congruence of triangles. Thus coordinate geometry provides a new method of analysis and proof. Coordinate geometry is also a base for the discussion of vectors, which are becoming increasingly important in mathematics.

SOLID GEOMETRY

It has been proposed for a generation or more that solid geometry become a part of the tenth grade geometry course. The new experimental programs have finally made the change. The present geometry course includes material from solid geometry, such as:

Planes and intersections of lines and planes.
Parallel planes and perpendicular planes.
Dihedral and polyhedral angles.

Polyhedrons, prisms, pyramids, parallelepipeds.
Cylinders and cones.
Spheres, spherical triangles, zones.
Volume and lateral area of solids.
Coordinates in three-dimensional space.

Since limited time is available for the study of these ideas, very few proofs are included. The topics are largely limited to facts about three-dimensional space.

However, there is considerable variation in the presentation of this space geometry. Some programs weave it in with the geometry of the plane. For example, parallel planes are discussed along with parallel lines, and spheres are an extension of the discussion of circles. There are other programs that treat the space geometry only intuitively with plane geometry and concentrate on the development of space geometry as a separate topic.

PROOF AND SYMBOLIC LOGIC

Traditionally, high-school students have received their first exposure to formal proof in mathematics in the geometry course. In the new courses students are expected to prove certain theorems in algebra as well. But even now no other course has as large a diet of proof as the geometry course. For this reason, many of the geometry courses explore the nature of proof and symbolic logic.

The question of proof has always baffled students in mathematics, particularly students of geometry, where, as we have said, the proving of theorems has made up a large part of the course. Students wonder why it is necessary to spend so much time proving things which seem quite obvious. Why, for example, must one prove that if two lines, $\overleftrightarrow{AB}$ and $\overleftrightarrow{CD}$, intersect at point E, the vertical angles formed have equal measures?

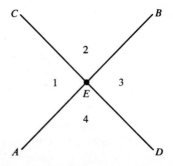

Why not simply measure the angles and then state without further ado that angle 1 has the same measure as angle 3, and angle 2 has the same measure as angle 4?

This question goes directly to the heart of mathematics. Mathematics differs from other sciences in that it is not an experimental science. In physics, the scientist forms an hypothesis, performs a number of experiments, and then states whether his hypothesis is true or not. (This description of the scientific method is considerably oversimplified, but essentially it is correct.) The mathematician, on the other hand, must prove his hypothesis by means of deductive logic before it can be accepted as true. In 1742, a Russian mathematician named Christian Goldbach had the idea that every even number is the sum of two primes: for example, $8 = 5 + 3$; $10 = 7 + 3$; $22 = 19 + 3$. No mathematician has ever been able to find an even number that is *not* the sum of two prime numbers. But, on the other hand, no mathematician, including Goldbach, has ever been able to prove deductively that his idea is correct. Without such a proof, it is entirely possible, though not likely, that one day a mathematician will actually find an even number that is *not* the sum of two primes. Consequently, Goldbach's notion is accepted only as an hypothesis, a conjecture, not as a theorem; and until it is proved deductively, it will remain known as Goldbach's conjecture.

What is new about proof in high-school geometry is that while it continues to use the method of deductive proof, it explores the nature of proof, rather than, as formerly, accepting it without analysis. The tool that plays an important part in exploring the nature of proof is *symbolic logic.*

Symbolic logic itself is a new development in mathematics. Interestingly, one of the important contributors to symbolic logic is the English mathematician Charles Lutwidge Dodgson, who is better known to the world as Lewis Carroll, the author of *Alice in Wonderland.* Although symbolic logic is as much a part of philosophy as it is of mathematics, its usefulness in mathematics is undisputed in making clear the rules of inference and deductive reasoning.

In constructing a proof it is necessary to use statements. In symbolic logic, as in much of mathematics in general, the statements are represented by symbols. Let us take as an example three simple statements:

> It is snowing.
> It is cold.
> We will go skiing.

These sentences can be combined in various ways to make compound statements, such as:

> It is snowing, *and* it is cold.
> It is snowing, *or* it is cold.
> *If* it is snowing, *then* we will go skiing.

Working with these statements in the form of words proves to be complicated in mathematics, so we find a way to represent the statements and the relationships between them by certain symbols. Suppose we assign to each of our simple statements a letter, as follows:

Statement	*Symbol*
It is snowing.	p
It is cold.	q
We will go skiing.	r

Now we need symbols to indicate the relationships among the simple statements when they are used to form compound sentences. This table indicates such symbols, as used in various compound statements:

Compound Sentences	*Symbols*
It is snowing *and* it is cold.	$p \wedge q$
It is snowing *or* it is cold.	$p \vee q$
If it is snowing, *then* we will go skiing.	$p \rightarrow q$
It is *not* snowing.	$\sim p$
If it is snowing *and* it is cold, *then* we will go skiing.	$(p \wedge q) \rightarrow r$

In these symbolic sentences, we use $\wedge$ to represent "and." The compound sentence $p \wedge q$ is called a *conjunction*. The symbol $\vee$ is used to represent "or," and the compound sentence $p \vee q$ is called a *disjunction*. The arrow symbol $\rightarrow$ represents an "if-then" statement, and the compound sentence $p \rightarrow r$ is called an *implication*. Finally, the negative of a statement is represented by $\sim$.

Suppose we make this series of statements:

1. If it is snowing, then it is not cold.
2. If it is not cold, then we will go skiing.
3. Therefore, if it is snowing, we will go skiing.

We can now write this sequence of statements in symbols like this:

1. $p \rightarrow \sim q$
2. $\sim q \rightarrow r$
3. Therefore, $p \rightarrow r$

Let us see how the chain of statements in a proof works in the case of the geometric theorem we mentioned earlier; namely, the vertical angles formed by intersecting lines have equal measure. In other words, in the diagram below, angle 1 has the same measure as angle 3 and angle 2 has the same measure as angle 4.

Let p represent the sentence $\overleftrightarrow{AB}$ and $\overleftrightarrow{CD}$ are straight lines.

Let q represent the sentence   The measures of angles 1 and 2 total 180, and the measures of angles 2 and 3 total 180.

Let r represent the sentence   The sum of the measures of angles 1 and 2 equals the sum of the measures of angles 2 and 3.

Let s represent the sentence   The measure of angle 1 equals the measure of angle 3.

In symbols the sequence of statements is represented like this:

1. $p \rightarrow q$
2. $q \rightarrow r$
3. $r \rightarrow s$
4. Therefore, $p \rightarrow s$

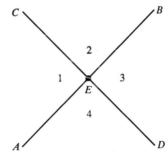

The chain of statements in a proof of an algebraic equation follows this same pattern:

Let p represent the sentence $3x + 7 = 22$
Let q represent the sentence $3x = 15$
Let r represent the sentence $x = 5$

166 *The New Mathematics in Our Schools*

Now we can write the proof for the compound statement "If $3x + 7 = 22$, then $x = 5$." The algebraic proof looks like this.

1. If $3x + 7 = 22$, then $3x = 15$. $p \rightarrow q$
2. If $3x = 15$, then $x = 5$. $q \rightarrow r$
3. If $3x + 7 = 22$, then $x = 5$. $p \rightarrow r$

The sentences used in logic are either true or false but not both. In order for the conclusion to a chain of statements to be true, each statement of the argument must be true. Usually the reason statements are true is that they are definitions, assumptions, or previously proved statements.

Determining the truth value of a sentence corresponds to finding the truth set for an equation. The equation $3x + 7 = 22$ is true if $x = 5$.

The simplest determination of the truth value of a statement is that for negation:

If it is true that "It is snowing" then the statement "It is not snowing" is false.

If it is not true that "It is snowing" then the statement "It is not snowing" is true.

We summarize these results in a table called a *truth table*.

NEGATION

p	$\sim p$
T	F
F	T

Next let's find the truth table for the conjunction "It is snowing *and* it is cold," or $p \wedge q$. The conjunction "and" suggests that both conditions are true at the same time. Hence, we will want the truth of a conjunction to mean that the compound sentence is true only when both of the original sentences are true. This gives us these truth values:

1. When it is snowing and it is cold, then $p \wedge q$ is true.
2. When it is snowing and it is not cold, then $p \wedge q$ is false.

3. When it is not snowing and it is cold, then $p \wedge q$ is false.
4. When it is not snowing and it is not cold, then $p \wedge q$ is false.

The truth table is the following:

CONJUNCTION

p	q	$p \wedge q$
T	T	T
T	F	F
F	T	F
F	F	F

In the table we think of p and q as placeholders for statements. Then $p \wedge q$ is an open statement much as the equation $3x + 7 = 22$ is an open statement. The sentence $3x + 7 = 22$ is true if $x = 5$. The conjunction $p \wedge q$ is true only when p is true and q is true.

For the statement, $p \vee q$, the disjunction is true if either p or q or both are true. These conditions give us this truth table:

DISJUNCTION

p	q	$p \vee q$
T	T	T
T	F	T
F	T	T
F	F	F

The only time this compound statement is false is when both statements are simultaneously false.

The truth table for $p \rightarrow r$ is a little tricky. Suppose that your friend makes the statement "If it is snowing, then we will go skiing." Under what conditions will you be disappointed with your friend? You would be satisfied that your friend is keeping his word if:

1. It is snowing and you go skiing.
2. It is not snowing and you go skiing.
3. It is not snowing and you do not go skiing.

The only time you think your friend has deceived you is if

4. It is snowing and you do not go skiing.

This suggests the following truth table for $p \rightarrow r$:

IMPLICATION

p	r	$p \rightarrow r$
T	T	T
F	T	T
F	F	T
T	F	F

Thus the only time the implication $p \rightarrow r$ is false is if p is true and r is false.

Another way to analyze mathematical situations logically is to use Venn diagrams. For example, they are useful in showing the relationships between different sets of numbers, as follows:

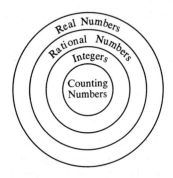

Here is an example of the relationship of Venn diagrams and sets to a simple proof.

Let P = the set of persons living in Los Angeles.
     Q = the set of persons living in California.
     R = the set of persons living in the United States.
Let p represent "a person living in Los Angeles."
    q represent "a person living in California."
    r represent "a person living in the United States."

Then the Venn diagram is:

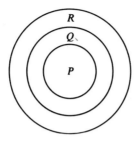

The subset relations are: *P* is a subset of *Q*.
                          Q is a subset of *R*.
                          Therefore, *P* is a subset of *R*.

The steps of a logical argument are:

Statements	*Symbolic Sentences*
1. If a person lives in Los Angeles, then he lives in California.	1. $p \rightarrow q$
2. If a person lives in California, then he lives in the United States.	2. $q \rightarrow r$
3. Therefore, if a person lives in Los Angeles, then he lives in the United States.	3. $p \rightarrow r$

This relationship is sometimes stated in the form of a syllogism, as follows:

Major premise: All Los Angeles residents live in California.
Minor premise: All California residents live in the United States.
Conclusion: All Los Angeles residents live in the United States.

Of course, not all relationships are as straightforward as this; for example:

Major premise: Some men are intelligent.
Minor premise: Some animals are intelligent.

Is the conclusion "intelligent animals are men" true? Let us try to answer this question with Venn diagrams.

The Venn diagrams may be

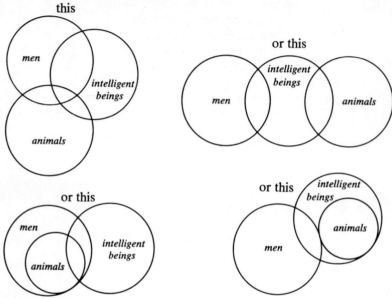

Thus Venn diagrams cannot be used to prove logically the truth of some conclusions.

EXERCISES

1. The letters *p*, *q*, and *r* represent the statements

   p = Today is Independence Day.
   q = It is a warm day.
   r = I will play golf.

   Translate these symbolic sentences into words.

   a. $\sim r$
   b. $p \wedge r$
   c. $p \vee r$
   d. $p \to r$
   e. $(p \wedge r) \to q$

2. Draw the Venn diagrams for these situations.

   a. All dogs are animals.
      Porky is a dog.
   b. Some girls are beautiful.
      Joan is a girl.

      c. Some boys are intelligent.
         Some girls are intelligent.
      d. All mathematicians are intelligent.
         All seniors are intelligent.
      e. Some parents are clever.
         Some parents are mathematicians.

3. Complete this truth table for $\sim q \rightarrow \sim p$.

p	q	$p \rightarrow q$	$\sim q$	$\sim p$	$\sim q \rightarrow \sim p$
T	T	T			
T	F	F			
F	T	T			
F	F	T			

UNRESOLVED ISSUES

11

We have now come to the end of this brief tour of the new mathematics, and we trust that you have an appreciation of its content, its spirit, its objectives, and its special point of view. Perhaps you will not remember all of the details of every topic that was discussed in the preceding chapters, but we hope that you have acquired an understanding of modern mathematics' concern with basic mathematical ideas, underlying principles, and the unity of mathematics. Hopefully, modern mathematics no longer seems so outlandish to you as it did when you first examined your child's new mathematics textbook or were first asked by him to help with his homework in mathematics. Hopefully, too, you can appreciate how remarkable mathematics is as an intellectual discipline.

But it is entirely possible that you still have some lingering doubts about the appropriateness of the new mathematics programs. It is understandably difficult for an adult to revise his long-held notions about a subject and accept a new version with immediate, unrestrained enthusiasm. Perhaps your youngster's own enthusiasm for his work in mathematics will gradually remove whatever doubts remain in your own mind.

Actually, we should examine the evidence at hand and use good judgment in our acceptance of the new programs. As a nation, we would be foolish indeed if we permitted ourselves to accept without question any new curriculum, no matter how positive and enthusiastic its creators may be. It is no secret that many school systems have yielded to outside pressures in installing the new programs, in order to jump on the mathematics bandwagon. Not all school systems have used good judgment in installing the new courses. Some schools have probably moved too quickly into the new programs, asking teachers to handle them without having made proper provision for training them in the new courses. Some programs have been accepted without asking where they lead or for whom they were designed.

It is no wonder, then, that significant questions have been raised about certain aspects of these programs. One need not be considered an enemy of the new mathematics to raise questions about the programs. Many proponents of the new programs, even including some of their creators themselves, are willing to admit that all may not be perfect in this new world of mathematics.

What are some of these significant questions?

First, do we really know which mathematical topics can be most effectively developed at a given grade level? Experimental programs have shown that sophisticated ideas can be learned by young children. Anyone who has seen, for example, a lesson in an intuitive approach to quadratic equations taught to a fifth-grade class by Dr. Robert Davis, founder of the Madison Project, can only marvel at the ability of the youngsters to grasp the ideas presented in the space of a single class period. But is this reason enough to include the subject in the fifth-grade curriculum? The new programs have consistently pushed topics formerly taught in one grade down a year or more below that grade. Does the fact that a certain topic *can* be taught necessarily mean that it *ought* to be taught? This question arouses sharp differences of opinion. Some educators believe that youngsters deserve to be taught as much as they can possibly absorb, and to do otherwise is to deny them a fundamental educational right. Furthermore, say these educators, our world becomes more and more complicated. Our children will have to know considerably more about mathematics— and at an earlier age—than we have been willing to let them know in order to cope with this world. In 1963 a conference of mathematicians, mathematics educators, mathematics users, and psychologists met in Cambridge, Massachusetts, to consider a new framework for mathematics education. One of the most important outcomes of this Cambridge conference was a recommendation that the "ideal" mathematics program would be one which would complete by grade 6 work now not studied until the third year of high school and which by grade 12 would have covered work that is the equivalent of three years of present-day college mathematics. By grade 12 the college-bound student would be expected to have mastered the equivalent of two years of calculus and one semester each of modern algebra and probability theory.

The report of the Cambridge conference was met with equal degrees of enthusiastic advocacy and startled consternation. Debate waxed hot—and still does—about its recommendations. Administrators who were still struggling to get their modern mathematics courses off the ground have wondered what changes would next be expected of them.

But the issue still remains: should we move in the direction of the Cambridge report's recommendations or would we be better advised to make sure that what we teach is well taught to pupils who can master the ideas and skills involved. To answer this we must have clearly in mind the goals we are striving to attain. What do we want our children to know? How does a student who has become competent differ in his behavior from the student who has not reached this goal? What is an ideal product of our schools? Only when we answer questions such as these can we rate the quality of a new program. Only when we relate content to outcomes can we render good judgment in evaluating the content.

A second important issue concerns the question of which of the new topics should become a permanent part of the new mathematics curriculum. Are we wise, for example, in spending as much time as some programs do on numeration systems in various bases? Is it necessary for youngsters beginning in grade one to learn how to operate in base five, base two, base eight, as well as base ten? Certainly, to adults who have been base-ten bound for almost all of their lives, the notion of operating in another base is intriguing. But perhaps there are other ways to build an understanding of numeration and computation. Perhaps there are topics that are not now taught which might achieve the same purpose. Here, clearly, is an area where some clear-headed research is needed.

Then there is the question of emphasis on structure in mathematics. How fruitful is it for so much stress to be placed on the basic axioms of our number systems, such as commutativity, associativity, distributivity? And if these basic ideas are to be taught, what is the best time to teach them? Some educators believe that youngsters must have many years of experience with numbers before they can truly comprehend the significance of these principles. Others say that these ideas must be brought to the fore early so that youngsters might be fully conscious at all times of how the wheels of the number systems go round. Still others say that teaching these principles at all is a complete waste of time. After all, they point out, mathematics is like a building. A building is meant to be lived in and worked in; one does not spend one's time boasting about the high quality of the foundation. To this the advocates of teaching structure reply hotly that one really does not understand the nature of mathematics unless he can appreciate these deeply embedded principles. Mathematics, they say, is an abstract structure, a model for thinking, and the earlier one recognizes this the sooner can one cope with mathematics.

Related to this problem is another: what degree of rigor or mathematical precision in definitions and proofs is appropriate at various grade levels? Should mathematical ideas be presented in language that may be simple, yet, by virtue of its simplicity be somewhat lacking in exactness? Hopefully common sense will prevail here and mathematics will heed the admonition, "Sufficient unto the day is the rigor thereof." In other words, what may be rigorous for grade three need not be considered rigorous in grade nine. Certainly, we have not heard of any mathematics curriculum maker who would advocate, for example, that before youngsters in grade two can work with counting numbers they must understand the Peano postulates upon which the number system is based. Discussion of these postulates might be reserved for the high-school years. But then again, there are those who would say that any discussion of the Peano postulates below the college level is pointless.

Another aspect of this problem concerns the language that is to be used in presenting mathematical ideas. What vocabulary and symbolism are appropriate? The Peano postulates come to mind again as an example in this connection. You will recall that Peano stated in effect that every natural number has a successor—that the successor of 1 is 2, the successor of 2 is 3, and so on. This idea, stated in this sort of informal language, would certainly be clear even to an elementary-school youngster. But Peano carried his logical processes much further. He used his postulate regarding consecutive numbers to define addition. He said that addition on the natural numbers is a binary operation designated by the symbol $+$ for which

$$1 + x = x^*$$
$$x^* + y = (x + y)^*$$

where x and y are natural numbers and x^* and $(x + y)^*$ stand for the successors of these numbers. This definition of addition is rigorous and mathematically useful. But this does not appear to be the idea of addition that ought to be presented to an elementary youngster. Virtually all curriculum reformers would agree that Peano's definition had best be left for later years of school, but the reformers have not always used the same degree of common sense in analogous situations.

In the same family of unresolved issues is the question of which applications of mathematical ideas should be included in school mathematics. The new programs include few applications to everyday life. If the traditional mathematics course went overboard in its concern with the use of mathematics in shopping, installment buying, insurance, and banking, the new programs, in their eagerness to get at mathematical ideas, have slighted the applications of mathematical ideas. Many curriculum reformers are already at work changing this situation.

But the problem may be somewhat more complicated than appears at first glance, for one must consider what is meant by "applications" and "everyday life." Do we mean only the world of the supermarket, the bank, the utility company, the lumberyard, the hardware store? Certainly these are part of our everyday life. But it could well be that if our applications were limited to such areas of utility, we would be giving youngsters trivial exercises in mathematics. Furthermore, isn't it true that our everyday world today includes as well the world of science, engineering, the computer? Shouldn't mathematics be applied in these settings as well? If the answer is yes, then one must consider the further question of how problems involving scientific ideas can be presented without having to teach not only the mathematics involved but the science as well? This is a challenging problem that some mathematics educators are diligently trying to face up to.

Another unresolved issue relates to the level of computational skill that should be expected of students. To many people knowing mathematics means merely being able to do a calculation like 24×16 rapidly and correctly. We have seen in this book that mathematics involves much more than skill in handling this kind of problem. But just where do computational skills fit into the total picture? Should computational skills receive continued emphasis? In the automated world of tomorrow based on electronic computers, will a student have to be as skillful in computation as the student of a generation ago? If it is agreed that computational skills are still necessary, what are the best means of helping students attain them?

It should be recognized that the new programs admit the importance of computational skill. The argument that these skills are outdated is a specious one. These skills are still needed, so that when a student is learning new subject matter, he can concentrate on the new ideas rather than on the computations involved. Furthermore, skill in the mechanics of mathematics is likely to facilitate productive thinking in problem solving and in research and creative activities.

The position of many of the new curriculum groups is typified by this statement from the *Program for College Preparatory Mathematics* of the College Entrance Examination Board:

> Strong skills are surely needed but they must be based on understanding and not merely on rote memorization. Once meaning has been achieved, then drill should be provided to establish skills—skills that can be performed, as Whitehead says, "without thinking." In this way, the mind is liberated to grapple with new ideas.

But there is some concern that in the emphasis of the new courses on ideas little time will be left for the development of skills. Some educators fear that this situation might develop with teachers who are not at home with the new content. Such teachers may have so much difficulty developing the new ideas that they find themselves with little time to spend on skill development. (On the other hand, one also hears the fear expressed that the teacher to whom mathematics has always meant only computational skill will find the new emphasis on ideas so uncongenial that she will spend almost all of her time drilling on skills.)

Another point of view holds that drill as such is incompatible with the spirit of the new mathematics—that the deadly nature of drill will kill off any taste for the new mathematics, just as it did for the old mathematics. Educators of this persuasion are looking for new ways to insure accuracy and skill in computation. A new and admittedly extreme solution to the problem is offered by the Cambridge report referred to earlier:*

> Lest there be any misunderstanding concerning our viewpoint, let it be stated that reasonable proficiency in arithmetic calculation and algebraic manipulation is essential to the study of mathematics. However, the means of imparting such skill need not rest on methodical drill. We believe that entirely adequate technical practice can be woven into the acquisition of new concepts. But our belief goes farther. It is not merely that adequate practice can be given along with more mathematics; we believe that this is the only truly effective way to impart technical skills. Pages of drill sums and repetitious "real-life" problems have less than no merit; they impede the learning process. We believe that arithmetic as it has been taught in grade schools until quite recently has such a meagre intellectual content that the oft-noted reaction against the subject is not an unfortunate rebellion against a difficult subject, but a perfectly proper response to a pre-occupation with triviality.
>
> We are not saying that some drill problems may not be appropriate for the individual student whose technical skill is behind, but we do believe

* *Goals for School Mathematics* (Boston: Houghton Mifflin Company, 1963). Reprinted by permission.

that this should be the exception, not the rule. We are definitely opposed to the view that the main objective is arithmetic proficiency and that new, interesting concepts are being introduced primarily to sugar-coat the bitter pill of computational practice.

We propose to gain three years through a new organization of the subject matter and the virtually total abandonment of drill for drill's sake, replacing the unmotivated drill of classical arithmetic by problems which illustrate new mathematical concepts.

In the long run, perhaps, the conflict between skills and ideas will prove to be illusory. If skills support the learning of new ideas and ideas make skill meaningful, there is no reason why a good program in mathematics should not accommodate both aspects of the subject.

The final unresolved issue that we bring up concerns the ability level of the students for whom the new courses have been designed. Are these courses intended for all students or are they in fact only for college-capable students? If the answer is that they are chiefly for the latter group, what is being done, or should be done, for the non-college-bound student? In what ways should the content of courses for these students differ from that for the college-capable?

As far as the new elementary school courses are concerned, our experience with them is yet too limited to be able to answer with any degree of assurance the question of the type of student for whom they are suitable. Officially these courses are intended for all students. Whether this intention will be carried out in practice remains to be seen. We may expect that students will continue to show the same range of ability in mathematics that they have in the past and that adjustments in the course content, method, and materials will have to be made to take care of individual differences. Mathematics educators are firm in their belief that the answer to the problem of taking care of slower students does *not* call for a return to traditional mathematics.

On the secondary school level, we have evidence that the newer courses are not suitable for all students. Early in its existence the SMSG recognized the problem and prepared a special algebra course for students who were not capable of college preparatory work. This course was characterized by the same spirit as was the standard course and covered most of the same topics. But it did so more slowly with simple language, easy problems, and in less depth; it was not in any sense a traditional course. Despite this SMSG course, the problem of preparing courses in modern mathematics for the nonacademic student and the slow student is only now beginning to be faced, and we may expect to see considerable production in this area in the near future.

There are also questions about the discovery method. Must all the ideas of mathematics be discovered by all students? Of course, this is impossible. How then shall the teacher know when to encourage his students to discover an idea, what students have discovered it, and when the student should verbalize his discovery? The search for efficient ways to develop ideas will need to continue for some time.

These are the major unresolved questions about modern mathematics that are being discussed by mathematicians and mathematics educators today. As schools acquire more and more experience with the new courses, additional important questions are sure to be raised. The most encouraging thing about the present situation is that the questions *are* being asked and ways to answer them being found. The American educational community has never been willing to think of its curriculums as fixed and immutable, and it is clear that the new mathematics programs will continue to change even as more and more schools convert to the new world of mathematics.

12

Finally, we wish to consider briefly the role of parents in the mathematical education of their youngsters. The role of parents cannot be overemphasized. It is the parents who fashion the future by the influence they exercise on their children. It is the parents who largely determine a child's interests, habits, vocational choice, and values. It is the parents who provide the setting, the stimulus, and the resources for a child's development and education. It is the parents who develop the three *c*'s—conscience, curiosity, and character.

The new mathematics programs have re-emphasized the importance of the students' attitudes in learning mathematical ideas. These attitudes include the interests, values, appreciations, and prejudices of the pupil. Research on the development of attitudes toward mathematics indicates that the parent is a key person. As parents we transfer our attitudes to our children by what we say, do, and think. One way to nourish a poor attitude toward mathematics is to say:

"I feel sorry for you, having to study algebra."
"No wonder you can't understand it, I never could get the hang of mathematics either."
"You'll never be any good in mathematics doing it that way."
"You don't need any more mathematics to run the business."

Instead we might foster a favorable attitude by saying such encouraging things as:

"Sure math is hard, but it's a powerful tool that has many uses."
"If you get the idea, you'll enjoy it, like winning a game."
"Keep thinking and you'll find the solution."
"Nobody ever lost a job because he knew too much mathematics."

Progress in mathematics requires that the child complete assignments, read books, think independently, and be curious about mathematical ideas. To help our child study we should provide him with the space, the time, and the tools which he needs for his lessons. If at all possible, see that the study place is quiet, pleasant, and comfortable, with adequate light and a reasonable temperature. And we should encourage our children to study at a specific time. Mathematics books, programmed texts, models, toys, slide rules, computer kits are learning aids which you could provide.

To promote independent thinking we should use good judgment in giving help with homework. When questions are asked about problems on homework we should first express interest. Then we should try to ask questions which will help our child discover the answer rather than answering the question directly. Having the child explain the problem itself to you makes him think about the situation in such a way that the solution may be suggested. If you too can't solve the problem, don't express disgust but rather enjoy the problem as a challenge, a puzzle, or a game. Help your child to accept the challenge of difficult problems. If the answer is obvious there is no satisfaction in solving the problem.

In order to nourish curiosity we ourselves should enjoy to explore new ideas. Whenever we find unusual news items, facts, puzzles, cartoons, or tricks related to mathematics we should express our pleasure in them by sharing them with the family. We should encourage our children to read recreational mathematics books, view TV programs which have mathematical or scientific aspects, visit science fairs, and use library facilities. There is a wealth of material about mathematics in pamphlets and books written in a language that can be enjoyed by children and adults.

Competence in mathematics also requires reasonable facility in computation. Rather than continue the drill activities of the arithmetic text, parents can set up competitions, number games, and mental arithmetic in a recreational setting. Many commercial games are available at school supply stores and toy shops. Guessing games such as Twenty Questions and Password, and counting games like Nim and Buzz are described in the publication *Games for Learning Mathematics*, published by Walch Publishing Company, Portland, Maine.

If your child has a natural talent for mathematics, be sure that he capitalizes on this potential. The demand for mathematicians and mathematics teachers is great and is likely to increase. As a parent you should encourage your child, whether a boy or a girl, to consider mathematics as a career. Watch the newspaper ads to learn the demand for mathematically competent persons. Visit the school counselor to find the best courses for your child. Study college catalogs to make sure that your child will have the background for the college of his choice. Explore the possibilities of summer camps, seminars, advanced placement, acceleration, or summer institutes for superior students. Encourage your child to participate in science fairs or to complete optional projects for his mathematics class.

If your child is having difficulty with his mathematics try to give him help at an early date. The sequential nature of mathematics tends to compound difficulties with topics taught in earlier grades. Remedial instruction may be available in the form of tutors, special courses, summer courses, or programmed texts. Consult with your child's teacher or the school counselor for the identification of the source of difficulty and for information as to ways of providing for deficiencies.

To make a contribution to your child's progress in mathematics, you need to be informed of the current trends in mathematics education. To do this, discuss your child's school activities with him. Study his texts. Continue to inform yourself about the new mathematics (see the list of suggested books on page 183). If your community has an adult education course on modern mathematics, join it. Most important of all, discover that learning mathematics can be a satisfying, pleasant experience.

SUGGESTED READING

Adler, Irving. *Mathematics*. New York: Golden Press, Inc., 1958. A colorful, well-illustrated treatment of the history and applications of elementary mathematics.

———. *The New Mathematics*. New York: New American Library of World Literature, Inc., 1958. A popular discussion of many of the new discoveries in mathematics.

Bergamini, David. *Mathematics*. New York: Time, Inc., 1963. A beautifully illustrated book about mathematicians, mathematical ideas, and applications of mathematics.

Courant, Richard, and Herbert Robbins. *What Is Mathematics?* New York: Oxford University Press, 1941. A scholarly treatment, but a very readable book on the nature of mathematics, its topics, and its structure.

Deans, Edwina. *Elementary School Mathematics*. Washington, D.C.: U.S. Office of Education, 1963. A discussion of the new programs in mathematics.

Johnson, Donovan, and William H. Glenn. *Exploring Mathematics on Your Own*. New York: Doubleday & Company, Inc., 1961. Readable presentations of many topics mentioned in this volume.

———. *Invitation to Mathematics*. New York: Doubleday & Company, Inc., 1961. Popular treatment of interesting topics in mathematics.

Kasner, Edward, and James Newman. *Mathematics and the Imagination*. New York: Simon and Schuster, Inc., 1940. A classic in its presentation of some of the dramatic sidelights of mathematics in popular language.

National Council of Teachers of Mathematics. *The Revolution in School Mathematics*. Washington, D.C.: National Council of Teachers of Mathematics, 1960.

———. *New Mathematics Programs*. Washington, D.C.: National Council of Teachers of Mathematics, 1963. Discussions and evaluations of experimental mathematics programs.

Reid, Constance. *Introduction to Higher Mathematics*. New York: Thomas Y. Crowell Company, 1959. A layman's discussion of some of the ideas of contemporary mathematics.

Sawyer, W. W. *Vision in Elementary Mathematics*. Baltimore, Md.: Penguin Books, Inc., 1964. An ingenious presentation of the ideas and processes of elementary mathematics.

ANSWERS TO THE EXERCISES

CHAPTER 4

1. a. finite
   b. infinite
   c. empty set
   d. infinite
   e. empty set

2. a. true
   b. false
   c. false
   d. true
   e. false

3. a. $\emptyset$
   b. U
   c. A
   d. $\emptyset$
   e. A

4. a. (a, b, c, d, e, g)
   b. (a, c)
   c. (a, e)
   d. (a, c, d)
   e. (a, b, c, d, e)

5. a. 4
   b. 6
   c. 7
   d. 2
   e. 1

6.

a.

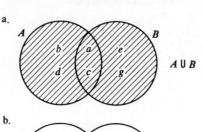

$A \cup B$

b.

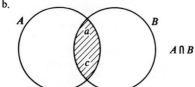

$A \cap B$

c.

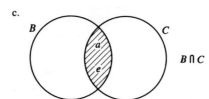

$B \cap C$

d.

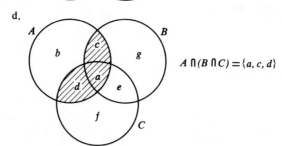

$A \cap (B \cap C) = \{a, c, d\}$

e.

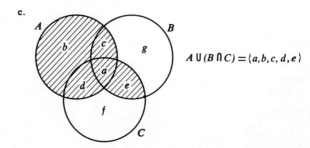

$A \cup (B \cap C) = \{a, b, c, d, e\}$

CHAPTER 5

1. a, c, d

2. e

3. a, c, d, e

4. a. yes
   b. yes
   c. 0
   d. none
   e. 0

5. a. $\dfrac{^-10}{2} = {}^-5$

   b. $\dfrac{0}{2} = 0$

   c. $\dfrac{2}{3} + \dfrac{1}{3} = 1$

   d. $\dfrac{2}{3} \times \dfrac{3}{2} = 1$

   e. $\dfrac{2}{3} \div \dfrac{2}{3} = 1$

6. a. $\dfrac{4}{6}, \dfrac{6}{9}, \dfrac{12}{18}$

   b. $\dfrac{^-2}{2}, \dfrac{3}{-3}, \dfrac{^-4}{4}$

   c. $\dfrac{10}{2}, \dfrac{15}{3}, \dfrac{40}{8}$

   d. $1\dfrac{3}{5}, \dfrac{8}{5}, \dfrac{16}{10}$

   e. $\dfrac{^-5}{8}, \dfrac{5}{-8}, \dfrac{^-10}{16}$

7. a, c, d

8. a. II
   b. I
   c. I
   d. III
   e. II

9. a. $x = 9$, commutative
   b. $x = 5$, commutative
   c. 4, distributive
   d. definition of division
   e. definition of subtraction

CHAPTER 6

1. a. true
   b. true
   c. false
   d. true
   e. true

2. a. 23
   b. 21
   c. 51
   d. 49
   e. 100

3. a. 33
    b. 28
    c. 1111

    d. 123
    e. 1213

4. a. 130_{five}
    b. 321_{five}
    c. 1243_{five}

    d. 14441_{five}
    e. 42_{five}

5. a. 10000_{two}
    b. 1010_{two}
    c. 1110

    d. 1000010
    e. $10100R1$

6. a. 121_{six}
    b. 402_{six}
    c. 131_{six}

    d. 140_{six}
    e. 51_{six}

7. a. $/, >, \triangle, / \cdot, //, / >, / \triangle, > \cdot, > /, > >, > \triangle, \triangle \cdot, \triangle /, \triangle >, \triangle \triangle, / \cdots$.

    b.

    c. 46
    d. $\triangle\ \triangle\ \triangle$
    e.

+	/	>	$\triangle$
/	>	$\triangle$	$\cdot$ $/ \cdot$
>	$\triangle$	$/ \cdot$	$//$
$\triangle$	$/ \cdot$	$//$	$/ >$

CHAPTER 7

1. a. 3 (mod 5)
    b. 4 (mod 5)
    c. 2 (mod 5)

    d. 1 (mod 5)
    e. 0 (mod 5

2. a. 7, 12, 17
    b. 10, 17, 24
    c. 11, 17, 23
    Other answers are possible.

    d. 11, 18, 39
    e. 21, 33, 45

3. a. $x = 4$
   b. $x = 6$
   c. $x = 3$

   d. $x = 0$ or 7
   e. $x = 2$

4. a. 5
   b. There is none.
   c. $x = 2$ or 4

   d. $x = 2$ or 5
   e. Each element of the set does not have an inverse with respect to multiplication.

5. a. yes
   b. yes
   c. yes

   d. E
   e. 0

6. One possible table:

*	a	b	c
a	a	b	c
b	b	c	a
c	c	a	b

CHAPTER 8

1. a. T
   b. F
   c. 0

   d. 0
   e. T

2. a. $5x = 20$
   b. $n + 16 = 42$
   c. $17 - a = 3$, or $a - 17 = 3$, or $a - 17 = 3$

   d. $2n - 17 = 5$, or $2n = 17 + 5$
   e. $8n = 96$

3. a. $\{12\}$
   b. $\{35\}$
   c. $\{7\}$

   d. $\{9\}$
   e. $\{1, {}^-4\}$

4. a. $^-1, 0, 1$, and others
   b. 6, 5, 4
   c. 1, 2, 3

   d. 15, 14, 13
   e. $(5, 5)(3, 7)(4, 6)$

5. a. $75 + 7$ is another numeral for 82.
   b. Addition property of equalities.
   c. Definition of division.
   d. 15 is another numeral for $75 \div 5$.

6.

a.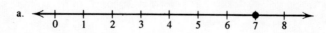

b.

c.

d.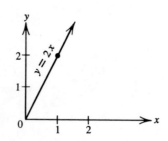

e.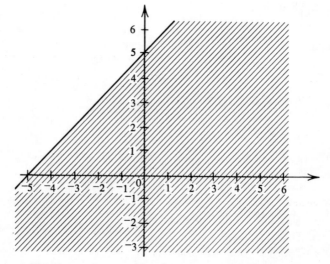

CHAPTER 9

1. a. 24
   b. 33
   c. 34
   d. 34
   e. $19\frac{1}{2}$
   f. 7.8

2. a. 12, 7, 8
   b. $a = 7$, $b = 9$, $c = 6$, $d = 11$, $e = 4$

3. a. 15, 18, 21
   b. 25, 30, 35
   c. 13, 16, 19
   d. 16, 32, 64
   e. 20, 24, 28
   f. 21, 26, 31
   g. 18, 22, 26
   h. 2, 1, $\frac{1}{2}$
   i. 81, 243, 729
   j. 48, 96, 192
   k. 16, 22, 29
   l. 9, 7, 8
   m. 10, 12, 13
   n. 27, 35, 44
   o. 2, 13, 2
   p. 25, 36, 49

4. a. $40 - 4$, 5×9
   b. 4×8, $50 - 10$
   c. 9999, 100,000
   d. 10000, $10 \times 10 \times 10 \times 10$
   e. 9876, $8 + 5$
   f. 10000, $90000 + 10000$
   g. 8, 3
   h. 444, 15
   i. 8888, 6
   j. $4/2$, 5×5
   k. 4, 495, 594
   l. 4, 999, 5, 5994

5. a. $4 + 3 = 7$, $3 + 6 = 9$, $7 \times 9 = 63$, $6 + 3 = 9$
      $1 + 5 + 4 + 8 = 18$, $1 + 8 = 9$, O.K.
   b. $7 + 8 = 15$, $1 + 5 = 6$, $9 + 2 = 11$, $1 + 1 = 2$,
      $2 \times 6 = 12$, $1 + 2 = 3$, $7 + 1 + 6 + 6 = 20$,
      $2 + 0 = 2$, Error
   c. $5 + 8 + 4 + 7 = 24$, $2 + 4 = 6$, $7 + 6 + 3 = 16$,
      $1 + 6 = 7$, $7 \times 6 = 42$, $4 + 2 = 6$, O.K.
      $4 + 4 + 6 + 1 + 2 + 6 + 1 = 24$, $2 + 4 = 6$

CHAPTER 10

1. a. Today is not Independence Day.
   b. Today is Independence Day and I will play golf.
   c. Today is Independence Day or I will play golf.
   d. If today is Independence Day then I will play golf.
   e. If today is Independence Day and I will play golf then it is a warm day.

2.

a.

b.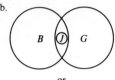

or

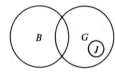

c.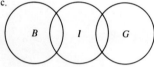

d. or or

e.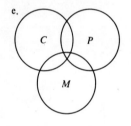

or

or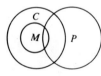

3.

$\sim q$	$\sim p$	$\sim q \rightarrow \sim p$
F	F	T
T	F	F
F	T	T
T	T	T

(Note: the truth value for $\sim q \rightarrow \sim p$ is the same as that for $p \rightarrow q$.)